MOTHER SETON
Saint Elizabeth of New York

MOTHER SETON

Saint Elizabeth of New York

(1774-1821)

LEONARD FEENEY

Revised Edition

THE RAVENGATE PRESS

Cambridge

Originally published by Dodd, Mead & Company
under the title: "Mother Seton, An American Woman"

COPYRIGHT 1938, 1947 BY DODD, MEAD & COMPANY, INC.

COPYRIGHT RENEWED 1975 BY LEONARD FEENEY, M.I.C.M.

New material Copyright © by Leonard Feeney, M.I.C.M.
and Saint Benedict Center

LIBRARY OF CONGRESS CATALOGING IN PUBLICATION DATA:

Feeney, Leonard: "Mother Seton, Saint Elizabeth of New York"
Revised ed., originally published under the title
"Mother Seton, An American Woman"

BX 4705. S5 7F4   1975   282'.092'4 [B]
            vii, 212p. illus., ports.   21cm
      1. Seton, Elizabeth Ann, Mother (1774-1821)
      2. Sisters of Charity of St. Vincent de Paul

            ISBN: 0-911218-05-X (Clothbound)

            ISBN: 0-911218-06-8 (Paperbound)

                  75-23224

PRINTED IN THE UNITED STATES OF AMERICA

Foreword

The thousands of details, the long, slow study of facts and proofs, the careful consideration of the whole case, for and against, which have been going on for many years in the cause of Mother Elizabeth Seton, have been at last concluded. On the authority of the Vicar of Christ, Our Holy Father Pope Paul VI, we may now call her, officially and confidently, Saint Elizabeth.

The perceptive reader has no doubt already noted from the copyright page that this book was first written a few, quite a few, years ago. When it originally appeared, Mother Seton's cause had not even been officially introduced at Rome. The intervening years, however, have seen the Process move at an ever-increasing pace to the final climax: an American woman universally proclaimed a saint of God!

Many American Catholics have participated in this achievement: the most distinguished prelates, the priests and sisters of Mother Seton's own Vincentian family, and the humble men and women who have asked and obtained favors, graces and, in a few instances, miracles through her intercession. This has been a united effort, and it is one of the most profound joys of this writer's life to have contributed some small bit to the final triumph. I feel the same exultation of spirit I imagine a devoted political worker must feel when he sees his candidate win a hard-fought election.

In one sense the story of Elizabeth Seton has reached its culmination, but in another sense it is just beginning. Our Holy Father has given the United States a most wonderful bicentennial present—he has declared that one of our native daughters enjoys a privileged position before the throne of God. It remains for us to ask Mother Seton's intercession in our necessities, so that our prayer may echo from one end of the land to the other: "Saint Elizabeth of New York, Saint Elizabeth of all America, our own Saint Elizabeth, pray for us and for our country!"

L.F.

*Portraits of Mother Seton and her husband
appear opposite page 54*

Credentials

The modern biographers of a saint have a fondness for making him over to their own image and likeness. The modern tendency is to give a saint all the recognized qualities of "a good sport," "a thoroughly nice person to live with," "a very human, natural sort of girl or guy."

The ancient chronicler of saints' lives followed a different course. He figured that a saint was someone more exceptional than an honest-to-goodness, nice, human person. Of this latter kind we have plenty, thanks be to God! But the saint's business is to create a vent between time and eternity, between natural goodness and supernatural aspiration. He or she is not merely a noble character possessed of a number of sound, solid virtues; but rather a creature struck by the lightning of God's grace. And a person struck by lightning behaves, in the force of the impact, very strangely at times. Saints are neither conventional nor predictable. "Good citizens" are.

Elizabeth Seton is a saint, by the grace of God and the solemn proclamation of Christ's Vicar, Pope Paul VI. She is the first saint to be born in our country. Mother Cabrini was of course the first United States citizen to be canonized, but, as everyone knows, she was born in Italy. We may therefore call Mother Seton the first American saint in the American manner. There is a French manner, you know, and a Spanish manner, and—

I

very delightfully—an English manner. There are all sorts of manners in the Universal Church, because the Church is supranational and in the matter of her saints has no one set style, any more than she has an architecture, being capable of using Byzantine, Gothic, Romanesque, Rococo, even Igloo (when the Eskimos arrive) for the commemoration of Her most Sacred Mysteries.

But this is the twentieth century—the age of atomic power, and moon landings and a host of other scientific and technical discoveries. Why do we need something so outmoded and medieval as saints? Maybe in God's infinite wisdom that's just what this century does need. We've tried about everything else, and where has it brought us? In no century since the world began have so many millions of innocent people been slaughtered as in this one—usually in the name of some kind of "progress." We are surrounded by materialism and immorality, with the consequent confusion, turmoil, and bewilderment of mind and soul which they inevitably bring with them. Even the Church herself has experienced defections and disruptions not thought possible a few years ago. We should not, however, despair of the final outcome. Our Lord promised that Peter's barque would not sink, but He never said that faithful hands would not have to do some bailing from time to time.

As He has done so often in the past, why may not God again use the weak to confound the strong? St. Bernadette beheld Our Blessed Lady at Lourdes, and the Catholic Faith experienced a new revival in nineteenth-century France, to the complete consternation of the atheists and free-thinkers who had been assuring each other that it was finally dead. Elizabeth Seton has waited one hundred and fifty-four years to be canonized. Why, in God's providence, may not this be the time when the Faith will have a new revival in twentieth-century America? We do not know, but we may at least pray that it will be so.

Fourtunately, we do not need to begin this outline of Mother Seton's career by being apologetic. The facts —what she was and what she did—are most impressive. Shall I tell a few? Well, she was the mother of five children, the aunt of one Archbishop, the grandmother of another. Not enough? Then what will you say of her having been the spiritual mother of more than nine thousand nuns now alive? (And of thousands of others who have gone with her to Heaven?) In America today these nine thousand nuns direct and conduct Colleges, Academies, Classical High Schools, Commercial High Schools, Elementary Schools, Technical Schools, Normal Schools, Nurses Training Schools, General Hospitals, Tubercular Hospitals, Maternity Hospitals, Leper Homes, Convalescent Homes, Homes for the Aged, Homes for Working Girls, Homes for Dependent Children, Schools for Deaf-Mutes, Infant Asylums, Day Nurseries, Centers of Social Service Work, Indian Schools, Retreats for Nervous and Mental Diseases. These were all begun and fostered under the aegis of her direct inspiration. From her, as the pioneer teacher in the field, stem, directly or indirectly, all the Catholic Parish Schools in the United States: over 1,700 High Schools with more than 300,000 students, and more than 8,500 Elementary Schools with well over 2,000,000 students.

In many styles of dress, from the white cornettes of the French peasant women to the black caps of the Italian Widow, her daughters, her Sisters of Charity, enrich, protect and comfort our land with the holiness of their good works, the sacrifice of their lives and the power of their loving prayers.

I do not want to give my whole case away at the beginning, but it may be appropriate to mention here that 154 of her spiritual daughters served on the battlefields of the Civil War; 189 of her merciful virgins administered comfort and consolation to the American soldiers in the Spanish-American War. Don't you think there must have been some great spiritual force to start this avalanche of self-sacrifice and charity?

Or, if you are more impressed by social and historical achievement, Elizabeth Seton was the most beautiful debutante of New York in her day. Her father, Dr. Richard Bayley (her marriage name was Seton, her maiden name, Bayley), was the first governmental inspector appointed to take charge of the Quarantine in New York, and was also the first professor of anatomy at the medical school of Columbia University. Her stepmother was a Barclay, after whose family New York's famous Barclay Street is named. One of her descendant blood-relations was Franklin D. Roosevelt, the thirty-second President of the United States. "In my childhood," said Franklin D. Roosevelt, writing in 1931, when he was Governor of New York, "my father often told me of Mother Seton, for she was a very close connection of the Roosevelt family and her sister-in-law was, I think, my great-aunt. Her distinguished nephew, Archbishop Bayley, was a first cousin of my father, James Roosevelt, and they were very close friends. In our family we have many traditions of the saintly character of Mother Seton."

She began life as a Protestant, and was not converted to the Catholic Church until she was a widow with five children. God's ways are not our ways, but the leading vanguard of the Catholic Sisterhood in America, the Sisters of Charity, is the result of the courage and sacrifices of a one-time Protestant girl, a maiden, a wife, a widow, a convert, a nun. The set-up is rather extraordinary. It may be profitable for us to inquire into the details of this strange career.

In the great joy of having in the calendar of our saints a name to rank, we hope, in equal brilliance with such spiritual heroines as Teresa of Avila, Therese of Lisieux, Catherine of Genoa, Rose of Lima, Joan of Arc, Jane Frances of Dijon, Bernadette of Lourdes, Frances Xavier Cabrini of Sant'Angelo, let us review, in brief outline, some facts in the career of our own Elizabeth Ann Seton, "Elizabeth of New York," an achievement of holiness of the New World; an American Woman!

A Nightmare

The saints are given to us primarily for our delight and admiration, to aid us and comfort us. Anybody who thinks he could be a Saint Augustine, a Saint Stanislaus, a Saint Thomas Aquinas, a Saint Thé-rèse of Lisieux, if he had cared to, falls into a category of extreme arrogance. At least admit that none of us could have been Our Lady or Saint Joseph if we had "cared to," or, as the phrase goes, "if we had willed to." God's saints are primarily the result of His predilection, and only secondarily the result of their own coöperation.

If this is not borne in mind, we are apt to deny to the saints the excellence achieved by them apart from the pattern of sanctification which we ourselves could have followed. Thus, when a child is seen to be in tender years so responsive to the ways of the spirit as to blush, or weep, or be covered with consternation at the slightest fault against God's Holy Will, faults which most of us would be proud to possess if they were the worst that could be held against us, we are tempted to turn up our noses and call them "scrupulous," "prudish," or some other belittling epithet that reduces them to the measure of our mediocrity.

Some people have been "scandalized" at the fact that the Little Flower bemoaned a few moments of over-indulgence of her senses in the fragrance of a bottle of perfume. "How could God punish her for such an innocent fault?" was the question asked. The answer is that

God would not punish her at all. It was she who put such demands on her own nature in virtue of her love for God. If I had a friend who burst into tears because of having failed to give me some delicate attention, the lack of which I could easily have forgiven, I should feel that this was not only a friend, but a most exquisite loved one of my heart. The choice between the *good* and the *bad* is the measure of salvation, and it is terrifying, but not strictly tragic. The measure of sanctity is the choice between the *good* and the *best!* To give what need not have been given except for love's reasons; to do more than was strictly required; to wish to be perfect and then strive for it by way of counsel, not of commandment; that is the saint's goal. And this choice is tragic to the last degree, the giving up of a loved thing or a loved person for the love of God. Only they know the poignancy of this choice, the choice of renouncement, who have essayed it. Let us not bring these exquisite souls to the level of our commonplace courage. Economic proletarianism is dismal enough. But a proletarianism of the spirit would oust from the Church every martyr, confessor, virgin. There would then be nobody to pray to or admire. Everyone would have been diminished to the stature of our own inferiority.

Elizabeth Ann Bayley was born in New York City on August 28, 1774, one year before the outbreak of the Revolutionary War. Her parents were of mixed French and English ancestry, Richard Bayley descending from a distinguished English lineage, combined with some French Huguenot blood that immigrated to America in the seventeenth century. Her mother was the daughter of an

Episcopalian minister, with ancestral roots in England. This pair had three children, all girls: Mary, Elizabeth Ann, and Catherine, in that order.

Of the favoritism of parents for their children, there is no rule, no prognostication. Some say fathers love their daughters most, mothers their sons. What can a man do who has only daughters? Love them all? I suppose so. But if there is anything certainly true in Richard Bayley's life it is that his favorite daughter was not, traditionally, the oldest, nor the youngest, but rather the middle daughter, the subject of this biography.

Nature alone does not set up the pattern of excellence in the life of a child. Grace also contributes. In view of her future mission and vocation, Grace was at work in the soul of Elizabeth Bayley from the very start of her career. There is no formula for such things. God picks His favorites where He wills, and is never stumped by the stupid anticipations of men.

His middle daughter most won Richard Bayley's heart. He loved her most, and he understood her potential greatness in his own dismal way.

I say "dismal way," for he was no more or less than a Christian humanitarian, a good thing to be absolutely, a most inadequate thing to be relatively. For humanitarianism in the case of an exceptionally ardent soul, and such was the soul of his daughter Elizabeth, forms a *cul de sac* from which eventually an expansive spirit is unable to emerge. Humanitarians do good to others for the sake of their own fine feeling in the matter; saints for the sakes of their beneficiaries in the love of Christ. Humanitarians approach the diseased with a white coat and an antiseptic stick: witness Dr. Heiser in his *American Doctor's Odyssey*. Saints take even diseased Negroes to their arms, even kiss their sores: witness Saint Peter Claver in the holds of the slave-ships that arrived at Carthagena.

There is something annoyingly admirable about humanitarians, say what you will; and something terribly deficient. Her father was Elizabeth's counselor, teacher, ideal. Yet in face of all he taught her, at the age of eighteen she had thoughts of self-destruction. You see, if you give a child an impulse that is not rooted in a dogma, a truth, you create a psychological lop-sidedness that is likely to become disastrous. When will our modern psychologists learn this basic lesson?

Very well, at eighteen, and in the face of the most correct and proper humanitarian environment, Elizabeth Bayley began to doubt the value of her own existence, whether to herself or others. But by the Grace of God this nightmare quickly passed. There is, as far as I can discover (and I have searched most diligently), only one other crisis of this nature in her career. Humanitarianism, it seems, cannot rest contentedly in the doctrines of Christ alone. It must borrow from a wide field, because it is not a doctrine, but rather an ideology. And so Richard Bayley kept in his library, and put at his daughter's disposal, the works of such writers as Voltaire and Rousseau. Voltaire seems to have disturbed her not at all. But Rousseau did. And when she was married only a few years, Elizabeth wrote to one of her friends, saying: "Every half hour I can catch goes to *Émile*. Three volumes I have read with delight; and were I to express half my thoughts about it, particularly respecting his religious ideas, I should lose that circumspection I have so long accustomed myself to. . . . Dear J. J. I am yours."

The book referred to was Jean Jacques Rousseau's *Émile, ou de l'Éducation,* a book both attractive and insidious, capable of doing infinite harm to the soul of an innocent young girl. That the harm was not done, and that, without any spiritual direction, she gradually discarded Rousseau, and reverted to her quest for something in which her spirit could rejoice without the pride of disillusionment, is a tribute both to the character of the girl herself and to the intense impulse of Grace that was drawing her step by step to the goal God had intended and dreamed for her from the beginning.

Times without number, the daughters and sons of the most edifying heretics have had to face that division between the natural and the supernatural that has sometimes resulted in their conversion, sometimes in their undoing. The case of "the parson's daughter" who sneaks a forbidden book under her pillow when all her father's indoctrination in the ways of heresy has proved ineffective is probably the margin and measure of the extent to which Catholicism and its counterfeits differ in the effective sanctification of a Christian soul.

Mr. Monitor

During Elizabeth Bayley's childhood the American Revolutionary War was fought. But what is the use of commemorating the details of a war waged when one was a baby? Do you remember, if any, the wars that were fought when *you* were booing and cooing in the cradle? Wars pass over an infant's head like vapors in the night. And if, as it is asserted, a child does not reach the full age of reason until about the age of seven, it may be said of the Revolutionary War that it occurred wholly within Elizabeth's lifetime, but that it had as much importance to her as something that happened in the pre-historic age. I myself was born the night the *Maine* was sunk, and never gave the incident a thought.

Except, perhaps, she might have remembered (for she was then six) the miseries of the winter of 1780, when New York City was under siege, and between cold and starvation the inhabitants barely managed to survive until peace was restored. The city harbored many Royalists, of whom Elizabeth's father was one, but despite their allegiance, even these were under suspicion of the English authorities. Anything that resembled or could be taken for an American soldier was quickly either shot by a Redcoat or tomahawked by an Indian.

The fact that Richard Bayley's sympathies in the war were with England can be explained by the fact that he was a surgeon in the British army, and was loath to be accused of disloyalty to his duty as a soldier. But such were his qualities of character and learning that, when the American Independence was established, he was warmly received by the citizens of the new Republic and given posts of honor in the community. The war cost him no serious reversal of fortune, and the days of Elizabeth's girlhood were passed in extreme comfort. Her education was genteel, and she was able in her time, as a belle, to achieve rank in the most exclusive New York society of the day.

Elizabeth's mother, it should have been said, died when the child was three years old, and soon afterwards her father married again, a Miss Barclay this time, in place of a Miss Charleton the first time. Elizabeth came to love and respect her stepmother as much as is possible in such cases, but her father became for her henceforth pretty much of mother and father combined. Nor did he cease to make her the chief object of his affection and interest even when other children came to him in the second marriage.

Elizabeth was brought up in an age when a girl was given a distinctly feminine education, one that coincided in practically nothing with the training given a boy. She did not go in for heavy studies like science, business, accounting, and never dreamed of being prepared for one of the professions. Music, drawing, French, literature, sewing, dancing, housewifery, etc., were pretty much the curriculum allotted to her. In Elizabeth's case there was especial opportunity for developing her mind because she had ready access to her father's large library. She grew into books naturally, was, and was encouraged to be, an inveterate reader, and came to be acquainted extensively with religious literature, history, and most of the greater poets. She shied away from French and music, after some study in those subjects; but at her father's command (she could say truly in later life that she had never once disobeyed him) she resumed them and became proficient in both.

Whatever be the defects of an all-genteel education for girls (and it did probably hinder them somewhat in the matter of health, with so much in-doorness, such heavy dresses, and such water-logged bathing suits, etc.), it at least was based on the reasonable assumption that the functions of man and woman are totally different. It is a strange commentary on our age that there never has been so much talk about sex as there is in this day when the difference between the sexes is almost totally ignored.

Again may I burst into this book with an observation which the reader is free to accept or reject? It is my persistent conviction that one of the greatest horrors of our day is the way in which a girl and a boy are treated indiscriminately in the matter of education and environment. The sexes are not the same, and there is a mystery between them which neither gender can fully fathom in the other. Woman is, among other things, not the lover in the partnership of the sexes. She is the loved one. Her business is to be admired, to receive adulation, courtesy, care, compliments. She grows restless and unhappy when these are denied her. Sister, daughter, bride, mother, these are her functions. Operating in any sphere in which she can achieve some one of these four-fold phases of her nature, she is contented, relaxed, at home, herself. Outside this sphere, she is an easy prey for dark complexities and nervous glooms.

There was in the old-fashioned girl something that needed to be liberated, chiefly, I should say, in the matter of her clothes. But the liberation has gone altogether too far. And if you find your subway companion elbowing his fellow lady-passenger out of a seat and letting her hang on a strap from the Bowery to the Bronx, you may get at the profundities of this discourtesy by paying some attention to what I have adumbrated in this interlude.

To Richard Bayley's credit be it said that his daughter was his daughter, not his son. And his moral training of her was flawless. Everything that was fine in the way of natural virtue he strove to inculcate, even to curbing excessive exuberance of spirits, which, in an affectionate nature, is a necessary astringent. Under his discipline, reasonably lenient, judiciously severe, there developed in Elizabeth's character, as Madame De Barberey has remarked, that happy combination of vivacity and restraint that makes a girl so thoroughly delightful.

"My dear daughter," he writes to her in 1793, when she was nineteen, "you will never deceive your father in thought or word. Let it be so, and if ever I do you, may I perish. Now live on, my child, let reason guide you; if your opinion wavers take always the prudential side. Ninety times out of a hundred we sacrifice prudence to our feelings. The object acquired in such a case seldom pays us an iota, but often brings a host of misfortunes with it. I hope you have made up your mind to laugh at all imaginary ills: it will smooth your path through life. Heaven be with you always. If your father could receive

additional comfort, it is at this moment when his daughter
writes that she is happy. But calm that glowing of the
soul, that warmth of spirits; impressions will then be less
readily admitted, but they will last longer."

In his letter to Elizabeth, Richard Bayley had a
habit of signing himself, "your father and friend." The
addition of "friend" is not admirable. Nor is the excessive paternalism that confuses duty to God with duty to
himself. "Heaven be with you always," though quite
innocuous, is the kind of phrase coined out of the heart of
heresy, which says "Providence" and "Goodness" instead
of "God"; a veering toward abstractionism that is in-
grained in all the sects. Nor did his daughter ever hear
her father pronounce the name of Jesus Christ until he lay
on his deathbed.

Nevertheless, there must be asceticism, which is the
law of restraint, before there can be mysticism, which is
the law of abandon. And the ascetical features of Elizabeth's training under her father's hand were praise-
worthy and salutary. For she was, like all of us, the vic-
tim of Original Sin. And if you think a nice little girl will
stay a nice little girl without the most strict surveillance
and discipline, you are reckoning with a nature other than
that given even to nice little girls.

What was lacking in Richard Bayley was a belief
consonant with his disciplinary régime. The discipline was
Christian, the dogma indefinite. Elizabeth needed to be
told, by way of heartening her in her penances, that a little girl just like herself once became the Mother of God.
She needed to know that the Incarnation was not merely an
opinion but a fact, and that the Body of Christ, wounded

on the Cross for love of us, has become, not merely commemoratively, but in substance and truth our Food. There must be an intense personal realization of the mysteries of Christianity, before the miseries of it can be supported. It was not until 1802, when she was twenty-eight years of age, that she was admitted to the Sacrament of— as they called it—The Lord's Supper. Twenty-eight years of age is a late day for a Christian child to be receiving her "First Holy Communion."

Nevertheless, in Dr. Bayley's case I think it was true that his love of God was deeper than he knew. Granted that God had seemed to mean no more to him than the *Dieu abstrait, sans lumière et sans chaleur* of his professed belief, there were times when the sheer goodness of his nature seemed to ally itself to Grace to effect a most touching display of Christ-like charity.

There is the pretty story told of him, how, seated one evening in the living room of his home in the Battery (the then fashionable section of New York City), a surgeon from Staten Island came to ask his advice concerning a critical operation. Though anxious to oblige, Dr. Bayley felt unequal to going to see the patient. It was late at night, the distance was great, he was exhausted from his absorbing engagements during the day. It was very dark, too, I imagine, in the ill-illuminated New York of long ago. And if there is one thing more than another that requires the most heroic self-conquest, it is to put on one's shoes again after one has settled into one's slippers for the night.

His fellow surgeon was disappointed. "How your refusal will grieve those needy persons who are so anxious to see you!" he said. "It will pain me very much to impart this news to them. They are already so unfortunate, and they are so poor!"

"They are poor?" exclaimed Dr. Bayley, jumping to his feet. "They are poor? Well, why didn't you tell me that before? Let us go to them."

> Ah Nature, framed in fault,
> There's comfort then, there's salt; . . .
> Dearly thou canst be kind; . . .

God makes strange alliances in the order of charity. Dr. Richard Bayley lost his life through ministering to poor, plague-ridden Irish immigrants, marooned in Quarantine in New York's port. It was in 1801. Sometime after his daughter Elizabeth's marriage, he had moved to a pleasant home in Staten Island. She used to go there often to visit him, and was on the point of bearing her fifth child, with her fourth child not yet weaned, when her father met with his death. Into the detention houses of the Quarantine several vessel-loads of these dear Irish had been dumped, lest they spread their infection, yellow fever, to the inhabitants of the city.

Elizabeth tells, in a letter to her sister-in-law, Rebecca Seton, what her father had to face!

"Rebecca I can no longer sleep. The dead and dying obsess my mind. Babes perishing on the empty breasts of expiring mothers. This does not proceed from my imagination; it is the very scene that lies about me. My father says that no one has ever seen the like of it. At this moment there are twelve children certainly doomed to die

from mere want of food. They are beyond the aid of sub-
sistence except that coming from their mothers' breasts.
But, alas! these unfortunates can no longer offer to them,
because they have been drained by the sickness which de-
voured them, while they were aboard. O God, Merciful
Father, how gladly would I give to each of these poor
little creatures a part of the inheritance of my own child,
if it only depended on me."

It was Elizabeth's plan to wean her own child in
order to give her breasts to those poor Irish babies in
their distress, but her father, with an understandable
prudence in the case of his own daughter, counseled
against it. But as a hostage for her, he did give his own
life.

One day in August, 1801, he entered one of the detention rooms of the quarantine where men, women, children, sick or well, taken from an Irish plague ship had
been crowded for the night, and this against his strict
orders. (He had left instructions to have the sick hos-
pitalized and separated from the others.) These poor
Irish immigrants had crossed the ocean in steerage. The
alien government in Ireland had persecuted them for their
Catholic Faith. By inhuman laws and practices, by famine
and complete destitution, they were exiled from their
own land. They arrived in America sick, faint, white as
ghosts. The sharp air of the new country, after the benevolent climate of Ireland, was too much for them. Many
of them had died immediately upon being taken from the
hold of the ship.

Elizabeth Bayley had more than once been struck
by the religious fervor of the Irish immigrants when they

were released from the ships and sent in to her father for
medical attention. She wrote of them: "The first thing
these poor people did when they got to their tents was to
assemble on the grass, and all, kneeling, adored our
Maker for the mercy; and every morning sun finds them
repeating their praises."

Well, Dr. Richard Bayley, noble humanitarian, saw
this last boatload of poor innocents in their utter distress.
He also heard them in their prayers, prayers such as only
the Irish can utter in a plague or a famine. Nor can it be
doubted that he heard them, their shy men, soft-voiced
women, and lisping children, in their prayers for *him*.
For what race has been more affectionately expressive to
the generosity of a benefactor? They called to Mary
and to Christ, and in the name of Christ—it cannot be
doubted—came Elizabeth's beloved father, friendly as a
friend, effective as a physician.

Upon entering the room I have described, on this
certain day, and braving the insufferable stench of the
air, Richard Bayley was seized with violent pains in the
head and the stomach. The infection of the disease of
these poor immigrants had caught him. Had also the infection of their Faith?

We do not know, except for this description of his
death, seven days later, written by his most loved daughter, who rushed immediately to his bedside. It is dated
September 5, 1801.

"No remedy could give him a moment's relief, nor
could he ever lie still without holding my hand. 'All the
horrors are coming, my child, I feel them all': this and
other expressions and the charge he gave me of his keys

convinced me that he knew the worst from the beginning.
No remedy produced any change for the better, and the
third day he looked earnestly into my face and said: 'The
hand of God is in all this: nothing more can be done,' and
repeatedly called, 'My Christ Jesus, have mercy on me.'
He was in extreme pain until about half-past two on Monday afternoon, the seventeenth, when he became perfectly
easy, put his hand in mine and breathed the last of life."

This was not the only time in the life of Elizabeth
Seton that a loved one would die with a hand in hers, and
in succumbing, mention for the first time the Holy Name
of Jesus, as we shall see. It seems to have been her lot
throughout life, both after her conversion to the Catholic
Faith and even in the years when she was groping about
for it, to have been almost miraculously effective at the
deathbeds of those she loved. Her presence seemed always destined to be a benediction to the souls of her dear
ones in their last agony.

Richard Bayley was, as we see, the kind of father
Elizabeth needed during the age of her life in which he
was with her. He had spirit, he had courage, he had
charity seeking an outlet into the realm of the Divine.
But his daughter, his Betty, more than compensated him
in this life for whatever he had done for her. For she
was indeed his *dimidium animae*, his *la douceur de ce
monde*.

Because of the high place she holds now in Heaven,
and because of the high honor of canonization, the highest
honor that can be granted to anyone in this world, Richard Bayley was very fortunate to have been the father to

such a daughter, and in the last breath of his life to have held her hand.

Be it also said of him that for all the intensity of his love for his favorite daughter, he was not a possessive father. No one welcomed more than he the advent into her life of romance and a husband in the form of young William Seton. His soul was too exquisite to make his father's love a monopoly of the heart of his child. He knew that the human heart can give itself completely in each of its approved relationships. There was a William Seton who received Elizabeth's heart fully in the function of a bride. There was another William Seton who, in the rôle of a son owned it no less completely. There were also companions with whom she communed in friendship to the fullness of her love. But Richard Bayley was her father; she, his daughter. This irrevocable relationship still exists in God's eternal summary of their lives.

Without Counsel

In the character of Elizabeth Bayley there was, from the beginning, a cast of holiness. She had a precociousness in the ways of the spirit, operating as it did only in the twilight of Christian truth. She was a bewildered moth, always searching for the flame, not sure where it was, but terribly sure *that* it was. Despite her spiritual discouragement at the age of eighteen and even her dabbling in Voltaire and Rousseau (it was not hers at the time to know of the Church's salutary *Index*), I doubt if she ever once offended God grievously. Her biographers, of whom I hope I shall be considered the least, have the happy advantage of being able to trace her spiritual development in every stage of her career, owing to her early-acquired practice of committing to paper all her spiritual struggles, chiefly in the form of letters to her friends; likewise there were from time to time entries in a journal, a diary, a set of "Remembrances." The candor of these personal revelations is authentic and unmistakable.

Whatever may be said of her training at the hands of her father, it is true to say that from her earliest childhood Elizabeth lived a life with God that was all her own. Though her father had in his solicitude protected her from worldly evil, it was not he who brought her to Christ, but she him. He gave her uprightness and integrity of character; but her holiness: her Grace-life, God-life, Christ-life, she acquired independently of him. It is remarkable to discern in the life of a child, compelled by circumstances to be something of a spiritual waif, not one instinct of bigotry. This not merely in the matter of nationality (she was willing, as I have said, to wean her own baby as a young mother, to give suck to starving Irish infants), but also in the matter of denominationality. Her religious adherence was to Episcopalianism. But her spiritual receptiveness was as large as Catholicism.

What will you say of her, all unbidden, wearing a tiny crucifix around her neck: a corpus on a cross, too, and this in the face of a religious training that dared not go beyond the cross itself (as though two juxtaposed beams of wood could have any spiritual value except for the death of Him to whose outstretched arms they were adapted as an instrument of torture)? Every time she heard the Holy Name of Jesus, she bowed her head, though this was decidedly not the religious practice of her associates. In sublime innocence she could not understand why they thought her queer in doing this. She grew into the habit of examining her conscience every day, making a most delicate account of her faults. And yet there was no mistress of novices to counsel her in these her tender years.

One would think that upon reading in medieval books about nuns and the conventual life she would recoil from them, as something that would be surely found among her own religious set if nuns had any value. Not so. She wondered, marveled why this peculiar feature of medievalism had been discarded. Nuns seemed to her to be so wholly beautiful, admirable. In one of her books she found mention of Guardian Angels, and henceforth was eager to have one for herself. The *Imitation of Christ*

delighted her, and the Bible so much so that she sought
to put into practice all the moral lessons learned from
the various stories recounted in the Sacred Scriptures.

It must be remembered that this was Elizabeth Bayley's own, private secret life, adopted without the instructions of her father or step-mother. Nobody asked
her to wear a crucifix. Nobody told her to bow her head
at the mention of the name of Jesus. Nobody exhorted
her to think that a nun-less Christian church was without
one of its strongest instruments of sanctification. And
certainly nobody coaxed her into thinking that the loss of
Guardian Angels among Christian children was a deplor-
able one. What did? Grace, and the predilection of
God's attuning her soul to supernatural dispensations?
It is quite possible to believe so.

She had an instinct for sacrament, as will be shown in
the touching account of her sojourn in Italy, when, in the
face of a sacramental observance she knew the Italian
Catholics were sincere in, she tells of how she went to
her room and held her own "little service" all by herself
with a book of the Psalms and a goblet of wine.

She had—and this is one of the hall-marks of sanctity—a thirst for mortification. Undisciplined human
nature is most gross indeed, as millions of disillusioned
couples learn every night in the brothels of the world.
Set, as we are, half in the realm of the animal, if the spirit
does not have its unobstructed way over the flesh, there
results a horrid two-wayness of impulse that disappoints
us each in each. Mortification is not only requisite for
salvation, but even for love or friendship of any kind.
Only, by mortification do lovers and friends remain faith-

ful to the end, in woe and weal. One must often marvel
at the mortification of spirit demanded in the marriage
ceremony of the Church. The priest does not ask the
beautiful bride or the handsome groom "Do you love each
other?" Rather he challenges them in terms of love's
disciplines. "Will you take this woman . . . for better
or worse, for richer or poorer, in sickness and in health,"
etc. This is love's language in our present exile.

Elizabeth Bayley was courted profusely in her youth.
Her physical beauty was compelling, but likewise her
spiritual beauty. The first without the second is disastrous, as our daily divorces will testify. Here is what
she commits to her diary concerning a certain M., who
thought her pretty and paid her courtship. Reflecting
that she might have turned his attentions to greater profit
if she had devoted herself more particularly to retirement
and prayer, she says:

"The consequences would have been, I would have
been pleased with myself; M—— would have been pleased
with me; even they to whom the sacrifice was made would
have liked me better; and, the heavenly consideration, my
God would have blessed me."

In a Christian curtailment of impulse (as opposed
strictly to the Oriental) the result is not bitterness and
pride, but rather tenderness and humility. In all Elizabeth's sufferings, and they were about as much, I should
think, as one woman could bear—in every sort of bereave-
ment, discouragement, abandonment, sickness—she was
never easy on herself, never relaxed for an instant into
any régime of idleness, laziness or self-indulgence. And
she loved solitude.

And what is it makes solitaries of the saints? Not a desire for loneliness, God knows. But rather because, in the most innocent places, the impulse to evil is found. It were not so had our nature not fallen in Paradise. Much has been said of the innocence of childhood, and too much could not be said, for we are not evil, and there is something beautiful in us that even Original Sin has not destroyed. But there is also something which Original Sin has definitely put there, and the first impulses of childhood are cruel as well as kind, selfish as well as generous. A child who is taught this (as all Catholic children are taught as soon as they reach the use of reason—at which point Confession must begin) is well armed against disillusionments, even among his playmates.

One of Elizabeth's earliest remembrances in childhood was of her girl companions taking some unfledged birds out of the nest and throwing them on the ground. She recalls how "she gathered them on a leaf, trusting that the little mother would come to them, and bring them back to life." She often cried, she says, "because the girls would destroy them; and at last, rather than witness their cruelty, preferred to walk or play alone." Life has a sinful secret. Would it had not to be learned so early!

Affair at Trinity Church

In appearance Elizabeth was small in stature, a model of slenderness and grace. Her features were finely cut, and her eyes a brilliant dark-brown. Her hair was abundant and went naturally into curls. A touch of French vivacity set off delightfully her English reserve. She was in a modest way conscious of her charm, as one ought to be. "I imagine my eyes were larger and blacker at that moment than usual," she wrote to her father in telling him of her joy at hearing one of his medical articles being praised by a distinguished French physician. The summer after her marriage, she sat for a portrait, in miniature; and her husband, writing to her from Philadelphia, says: "I showed my friends your portrait, and many agreeable things were said for which I felt greatly flattered, but let them know that the artist, although a Frenchman, had not at all flattered *you*."

Must one be beautiful to be a saint? Fortunately the Church puts no premium on physical beauty, demanding only beauty and integrity of spirit. But a beautiful soul will not be long in registering its excellence in the body with which it is associated in the intimate union of a single complete substance. There will be an "air," a grace, a poise in the material part of the saint that is the inescapable outcome of the spirit's dignity and peace. Ultimately there may be a halo.

Psychologically I think it is a help for a saint to be lovely in eyes and limbs as well as in virtue, because in the

acquirement of perfection ugliness is a hazard needing a
special Grace to compensate for it. It is often asserted
that physical beauty can be an incentive to pride. This
may be true, but I think not so strongly as the definite
absence of physical beauty can be an incentive to distraction; and the saint's soul needs the leisure of peace.

Not what has been achieved but what *is* is the measure of excellence I most admire. God, Beauty's Self, was
never *achieved* but forever *is*; and it is our delight to
know that Mary was *conceived* immaculate, never suffered sickness, nor even, after death, the body's decay;
likewise, that Our Lord was beautiful amongst the sons
of men and won friends and admirers by His natural loveliness and charm long before it was realized that these
had their roots in the deep springs of a Divine Personality. A sensitiveness to imperfection, which is the characteristic of all holiness, cannot be said *not* to extend to
every detail of one's person: witness the immaculate manners and dress of nuns in the elegant styles of poverty.
Ignatius of Loyola was not changed but supernaturalized
when he became Saint Ignatius. And yet it was he who
underwent several excruciating operations in a day of no
anaesthesia, in order to correct a defect in his walk.

I suppose the whole question is a speculative one, and
arguments could be brought up for the other side, but it is
not ungratifying to know that whenever a statue of
Elizabeth Seton is placed on an American altar the sculp-
tor will need to portray physical as well as spiritual
loveliness in our first aureoled one.

How many times Elizabeth Bayley was fallen in love
with, it is hard to say. But her destinies, in God's Provi-

dence, were set to be shared in marital union with a young New York financier, William Seton, who began to admire her when she was somewhere about the age of sixteen. At least in 1791, three years before their marriage, and when Elizabeth was seventeen, writing to his brother in the West Indies, he says, "It is currently reported and generally believed that I am to be married to Miss Bayley, but I shall think twice before I commit myself in any direction. Though I must confess I admire her mental accomplishments very much, and were I inclined to matrimony, not at all impossible, but I might fall in love with her; and I have no doubt but she will make an excellent wife, and happy the man who gets her."

"Happy indeed" we may say who know the event. But the condescension of this letter is understandable if we consider the character and the circumstances appertaining to the one who wrote it. To begin with, William Seton was, at this time, twenty-three years old, six years older than his bride-to-be. He was handsome in manner and bearing, as the portrait and miniatures of him show, one of which was executed by the famous Malbone when Seton was in his early twenties, and portraying him with the usual powdered hair, ruffle at the neck, and highbacked coat of the Continental cavalier.

He had a romantic beginning, having been born at sea, the son of a Scotch merchant who left his native land and came to settle in New York. How would we like, you and I—you who were born in Squedunk, and I in a place almost as bad—to have our births registered in the family Bible this way: "William Magee Seton, born 20th April, 1768, 35 minutes after 4 P.M., on board the ship *Edward*,

Captain Thomas Miller (long. 68.30, lat. 36). Baptized
8th of May, at New York. William Magee, of London,
and Elizabeth Farquhar, spinster, sponsors"? I think we
should feel quite rapturous about it and fall into the
habit of taking down the family Bible more frequently
than is the custom, even in the devoutest families.

At the time of the letter concerning Elizabeth,
quoted above, young Seton had been well started in business. Through the influence of his father, he had, for a
long while, the good fortune to serve as apprentice to the
Filicchis, a distinguished firm of bankers and ship-owners
at Leghorn in Italy. There he had come to know and be
intimately associated with the most élite of the grand
Italian society. He had also visited France and Spain.

With all this importance clinging to him, added to
the fact that his years were newly come to that very
"manly" stage in a fellow's life when young maidens seem
so ineffectual and silly; had traveled regularly on business in all the large American cities, and undoubtedly had
had eyes made at him by all the giggling belles in every
town he visited—it was not surprising that he assumed
at the beginning a certain superiority toward the Bayley
girl, merely in her teens, and that he hesitated to commit
himself as her suitor until she had become thoroughly
convinced of his magnificence. Furthermore, though managed with the most exquisite courtesy, it was an age when
condescension on the part of men toward women was the
rule.

Young William Seton was a good catch in every way,
but I doubt if Elizabeth made any real efforts to catch

him. To begin with, no record of their courtship exists,
and in her "Remembrances" written in her later life she
does not make a single allusion to it. Meantime we know
that during the years when she was being made love to,
she was entering in her diary spiritual notes and maxims,
analyses of her soul's state, that would do credit to a
novice in a religious order. I think it is certain that had
she been a Catholic at this time she would have chosen to
be a nun rather than enter matrimony. Social life, to
which she had ready access, seemed to have no attraction
for her. Sport (she was a skillful horsewoman) she
found equally unattractive. In the days when she was being wooed, she was avidly reading about the cloisters of
Catholic Europe, and once was half determined to run
away in disguise to search for some refuge of this sort
over the sea. Undoubtedly William Seton's strongest attraction for her when she first knew him was his ability to
tell her stories of the strange lands and peoples he had
visited and where her heart lingered.

It might be thought that the religious leanings and
ascetical practices of Elizabeth's early life would prevent
her becoming a whole-hearted bride. It does not turn out
so, either in her case or in any other I have known. No
one can achieve the rigorous generosity of marital love
who has not first been schooled in the rigorous aloofness
of virginity. Nor can a woman love man in truth until she
has first loved God. If any testimony were needed to
prove the exquisite and whole-giving quality of Elizabeth's love for "her William" as he came to be called in
almost every phrase, we have her letters to him after

their marriage, letters so incomparably generous and
tender that they might serve as models as exquisite in
their way as "The Sonnets from the Portuguese."

In the space of eight years she was to bear him five
children, proving she could be as generous as a wife as she
had been discreet as a girl. Hers was, therefore, and precisely because she was religious-minded and pure, a courtship in fact as well as in name. For love's first approach
is contemplative, not possessive, and courtship is the season of its purest delight. And love being most versatile
when it is chaste is driven perforce to all the devices of
chivalry: compliments, courtesies, preambles, gifts, even
verse and song. The young damsel of our own day who,
upon being introduced to a young male at a cocktail party,
allows herself directly to be dragged into a corner and
strangled around the neck, can hardly be said to be under-
going a courtship. Love once had an "art"; now it has
only a "technique." And the latter is monotonously un-
varied.

Of these two who came to be lovers, and eventually
husband and wife, there is no question as to which was the
greater spirit. Nor is this unevenness necessarily disastrous. Some of the greatest loves in history have been between a worthy and an unworthy person. Not that William Seton was definitely in the latter class; but he was
undoubtedly vain (the unpardonable sin in a man) and
somewhat spoiled. He knew he could have had almost
any girl he wanted for a bride, a disastrous attitude for a
lover. He had too much handsomeness, wealth, social experience abroad, which all must have made him strut
around like a pretty peacock in a New York that was

young and provincial. He was also in delicate health
which gives one the tendency to become babyish. Having
been spoiled before marriage, he needed to be spoiled
after it, and Elizabeth responded with complete generosity in this as in every other of his requirements. Yet
this cannot be laid too much to her credit, for to spoil
those in need of trivial, vain attentions is one of love's
most exquisite pleasures.

In a short time, owing to his ill health and reverses in
fortune, Elizabeth Bayley had to become mother as well
as bride to "her William," a service which beautifully
presaged the name by which she was to be known exclusively in her later life, and ever since, not "Mrs." but
"Mother Seton."

Well, it so happened that on January 25, 1794, at
Trinity Church, New York, Elizabeth Ann Bayley and
William Magee Seton became man and wife. Everyone
brilliant and distinguished was there, and the event was
quite the talk of the social season that winter. She would
not be twenty till the following August; he was three
months short of being twenty-six. Being Christians, they
both were, of course, united not merely in a natural con-
tract but in a Christian Sacrament. Whatever of them
was two in the natural order became one in the order of
supernature. They began at that moment to live as one
spiritual entity, and as one undivided reality in the
plan which the Eternal Father mysteriously had for them
in the name of His Divine Son. Whatever was strong in
the one began to be shared with the other and they participated in each other's Graces.

That William was honorable, loyal, charming, easy

to love, it cannot be denied. But the flaming spirit in that union was Elizabeth, the girl with the oval face and the large dark eyes whom he chanced to notice in her teens, and came eventually to prize more than all the donnas of Italy and demoiselles of France. He was an adequate, but indifferent, Christian. But her spirit would soon work in his, and her devotion would set him on fire even to sighing forth a beautiful invocation of the name of Jesus on his deathbed, just as her father had done under the influence of her prayers. This was her way, to inflame all she met with the contagion of her love. The social people of New York, seeing her going out in the early morning with her basket of medicines and food for the poor, could find no other name for her but "a Protestant Sister of Charity," a name as belittling of Protestantism as it was complimentary to the Church.

And so when William, and now Elizabeth, Seton walked down the aisle from the altar of Trinity Church on the morning of their marriage with the eyes of their admirers and well-wishers beaming on them, he was not then to know that the fine bones in the small hand that rested so confidently in his would one day be sought for as relics to be set in stone on one of the altars of the Universal Church of Christendom, or that the smallest shred of her bridal veil would be coveted as something sacred to the lips of the dying. Suffice it for him to have said on that happy morning, looking into her black eyes, enlarged, we may believe, "a little more than usual," and to have had the privilege of saying in truth, "My Elizabeth!"

Mrs. William Seton

It would be a grateful respite for us at this point, now that Elizabeth is married to the most sought-for of husbands, settled in a beautiful, indeed fashionable, home in the Battery, with wealth, health, social position, and eventually a houseful of children to comfort her, to lapse into the Jane Austen or Louisa Alcott manner and describe the charming domesticities and diversions of a pretty young wife. And I should not be in the slightest degree averse to following this course in my narrative were not the evidence so strongly against it.

It is true that many of these delightfulnesses during Elizabeth's first few years as a matron occurred. She grew more and more beautiful, her husband became fonder of her every day; she kept up a large correspondence with distinguished friends here and in England; her children were all safely delivered, all healthy, and all lovely to look at. She continued to be her father's most admired daughter, and in addition—and this is a great tribute to her charm—she was taken into her husband's family with as much enthusiasm as she had been cherished in her own. Because her in-laws were so numerous (William Seton, Sr. was, by two marriages, the father of fifteen children) being loved by them was equivalent to a popular acclaim. Only two years after her marriage we find her father-in-law writing to her as "my dear Eliza," showing her a packet of letters which his mother had written to him when he was a boy, urging

Elizabeth to "let no one look at them," and ending his
letter, a most admiring and loving one, with the salutation: "That you may long, very long enjoy every blessing
together is the sincere prayer of your affectionate and
fond father, Wm. Seton."

At his death, some years later, she was almost as
cast down as she was at the death of her own Dr. Bayley.
Furthermore, three of her husband's sisters, Rebecca,
Harriet, and Cecilia (six, thirteen, and seventeen years,
respectively, her juniors) became so attached to her
(they none of them married) as to never call her anything but "sister," kept up a constant correspondence
with her whenever they were absent from her side, supported her unequivocally in her conversion to the Catholic
Faith in later years; two of them followed her into it,
and all three died in her arms.

Indeed it can be said that in the first years of Elizabeth's married life there were not many dark clouds. She
describes her quiet Sunday, with a good coal fire in the evening and a volume of Blair's sermons for spiritual reflec-
tion. Her husband let her share in all his business interests,
thereby giving her the "What-Every-Woman-Knows" feeling. She tells her friend Mrs. Sadler, sojourning in Paris,
that "as for your Boulevards, I daresay they are very inferior to the pure air of the Battery," and can describe to
the same lady the much-praised beauty of her first child
Anna Maria, by saying: "Respecting a certain pair of eyes,
they are much nearer black than any other color, which
with a very small nose and mouth, dimpled cheeks and
chin, rosy face and never-ceasing animation form an object rather too interesting for my pen. Her grandfather

Bayley will tell you that he sees more sense, intelligence
and inquiry in that little face than in any other in the
world, that he can converse more with her than with any
woman in New York. In short, she is her mother's own
daughter, and you may be sure her father's pride."

Elizabeth had a remarkable ability at literary expression, a keen relish for and judgment of books, could
dance, played the piano beautifully, and in a circle of in-
timates in her own parlor could sing with a certain appeal.
All these are testified to in her letters, both sent and received. There was in her correspondence of affection with
relatives or friends no forced religiosity, and God was not
dragged in for others to witness in public display. All of
the qualities of the good old-fashioned girl that would
have delighted the hearts of our Victorian ancestors,
or given her the title to be heroine in a Civil War romance, were present in Elizabeth. And as a model letter
of such a type, we can quote a passage from this to her
father five years after her marriage:

"Should you be, in your retirement, unoccupied by
the cares and solicitudes that generally accompany you,
a letter from your daughter will be very acceptable; if
otherwise, it will be read in haste, and the idea, 'Bett is a
goose,' will cross your mind. I send it to take its chance,
hoping, as the children say, it may find you well, as I am
the same. It is currently reported that you are gone to
New London to inquire into the origin of the fever, and
that you are to proceed to Boston to see your children.
But I hope you will very soon return, and convince the
ladies who chatter on the subject that the origin is not the
object of your pursuit, but the remedy. . . ."

And again: "My dear Mr. Monitor: That you are
in the enjoyment of health in the midst of dangers, toil,
and death, is a subject of high exaltation to me; and if the
prayers of a good, quiet, little female are supposed to be
of any avail, it will be long continued to you, with the hope
that the visual rays of our fellow-citizens will in time be
brightened by your labors. . . . If you would sometimes
direct Helen's [her step-sister's] pen to Bloomingdale, it
would be a most grateful substitute for your own. . . ."
Wouldn't these passages delight the heart of a Mrs.
Gaskell?

And again, I offer this perfect tid-bit for the Evangelical: (after the mention of the coal fire and Blair's Sermons on a Sunday evening, quoted above) "But avast! I
am an American savage, I suppose, and should not mention such dull insipidities to a lady in the largest metropolis
in the world, and who can go and see blonde perukes on
Sunday eve and dance among the gayest. After all I think
the first point of religion is cheerfulness and harmony.
They who have these in view are certainly right."

All this surface gaiety might be skimmed from the
heart of Elizabeth Seton without one's ever realizing the
thunder, the urge, the stress, in a word, the Grace, that
was forever beating at the core of it. That is, unless you
took the time, at this very time, to read some of the documents she was writing for herself alone. The conflict in
her life, from the very beginning, was religious: that I
think nobody can deny if he will study all that has been
written. And the thing that was being done, with a cease-
less drive and insistence, was the abandonment of her
whole soul to the Infinite Love of God, through Christ.

Even her siege of melancholy at eighteen, and her fascination for a brief space with the *Émile* of Jean Jacques Rousseau, were religious crises, not secular ones. This is shown in the second case by the swiftness with which she abandoned Rousseau in favor of a more ardent embracement of Christian doctrine. (Father C. I. White, one of her biographers, believes, and rightly, that Rousseau's fascination for her came from Rousseau's clear proposals, in his sly way, of the absolute need for revealed religion, of which Elizabeth was having altogether too little.) Likewise her sense of discouragement as a young girl, as proved by her diary, was attached to the most eager desire to know more about the Christ she accepted implicitly in her heart, but in a too indefinite shape to be espoused as she wanted Him to be. A Freudian would disagree in this last point, and would reduce the symptom of melancholy to something psychological, or physical, or both, and the slightest measure in which he would be right (for we are not angels) would be the exact degree of precaution which should be taken of a young girl in her teens, to afford her both the proper surveillance and the proper tenderness. But the large measure in which he would be wrong would be his absolute inability to interpret the quality of her own statements in the matter, her worry about a "God who would have blessed me."

And if a much-courted, much-admired young girl may be said to be inhibited at the age of eighteen because she is not going to be married until the age of nineteen, then I leave the psychiatrists to their clinics. They may possibly find a remedy for the ills on which they concentrate by allowing free love at the age of twelve.

Nor can it be said that her father, her counselor in
religious as well as moral matters, projected a Christ-
complex into her life, for it was she and not he who was
the Christian. Indeed she sensed that it was but a trifling
amount of religion he had taught her, with the inference
that he had but a trifling amount himself. And I have
saved until now the striking incident that occurred at the
outbreak of his last sickness.

She knew (how did she know? she had no religious
preceptor but him, was only a perfunctory church-goer,
and was under the influence of no clergyman) that his religious ideas were altogether too conformable to a sort
of mild Deism. She knew that Deism is a thoroughly un-
christian attitude in which the human being works out
his own destiny with a certain placid nodding to God
when good form calls for it, and in its doctrinal void har-
bors a polite feeling of superiority toward the challenge
of Revelation. She knew that the soul of her father, that
spirit of which she said "it surrounds your child," was
not unequivocally a Christian one, and it drove her to a
wild fear that he would be lost—if it is through Christ
that we are to be saved.

Leaving his bedside, therefore, at the first crisis in
his illness, she went to the cradle where her fourth child,
Catherine, was sleeping, and clasping the infant in her
arms, and going out on the veranda where she could be
directly under the open sky, she raised the baby toward
Heaven, and made the following invocation: "O Jesus,
my merciful Father and God! take this little innocent
offering; I give it to thee with all my heart; take it, my
Lord, but save my father's soul." Such was the temper,

consistently throughout her life, of the woman with whom we are dealing. She makes a very bad "nice person" in any conventional sense. Her record is either that of a soul driven relentlessly by the urge of God to love Him and His Eternal Son above all things, or else it is the record of nothing.

Otherwise, how can we explain, at this period of which I am writing, why, in the atmosphere of loving friends, happy children, admiring relatives, and an adoring husband, with no worries, physical or financial, to harass her, we find her constantly retreating to her study to write in her private journal of devotions such intense prayers as this: "Almighty Giver of all mercies! Father of all, who knowest my heart and pitiest its weakness and errors, thou knowest the desire of my soul; it struggles to wing its flight to thee, its Creator, and sinks again in sorrow for that imperfection which draws it back again to earth. How long shall I contend with sin and mortality? When will that hour arrive which will free the troubled spirit from its prison, and change the shadow of this life for immortality and endless happiness? I bow to thee, my God! in cheerful hope that, confiding in thy infinite mercy and assisted by thy powerful grace, I shall soon arrive to that hour of unspeakable joy. But if it is thy will the spirit shall yet contend with its dust, assist me to conduct myself through this life as not to render it an enemy, but a conductor to that happy state where all mortal contentions are done away, and where thy eternal presence will bestow eternal felicity."

Of these and similar passages, in which there is indubitably much Evangelicalism, Elizabeth was to write, upon reading them after her conversion, "Oh, how different now. Oh, praise and eternal gratitude." Yet who shall have scorn for a spirit achieving as much as it was capable of in the days in which this diary was penned? God's arm is not shortened because the chosen one of His heart is confined, for the moment, in the dismal twilight of heresy. Upon the soul of Elizabeth Seton He had set His seal, and I should be prepared to affirm this even if she wrote nothing further in her whole life. But, dear reader, you have read nothing yet! Wait until you see what Elizabeth wrote on the boat and in the Lazaretto of Leghorn.

It may suffice to end this chapter with some excerpts from the letters she wrote to her own children, chiefly to Anna Maria, her oldest. Subjoined are the following as specimens of her soul's greatness:

My Dear Anna Maria:
This is your birthday, the day I first held you in my arms. May God Almighty bless you, my child, and make you His child forever. Your mother's soul prays to Him to lead you through this world, so that we may come to His heavenly kingdom in peace, through the merits of our blessed Saviour.

Again:

My dearest Anna must remember that our blessed Lord gave us the parable of the wise and foolish virgins to make us careful to choose our part with the wise ones, and to keep in readiness for His coming, which will be in an hour we know not of; and should He find us, dear

child, out of the road of our duty, like sheep gone astray
from their shepherd, where shall we hide from His presence who can see through the darkest shades and bring us
from the farthest ends of the world? If we would please
Him, and be found among His children, we must learn
what our duty is, pray to Him for grace to do it, and then
set our whole heart and soul to perform it. And what is
your duty, my dear child? You know it, and I pray God
to keep you in it, that, in that blessed day when He shall
come to call us to our heavenly home, we may see our dear
Anna in the number of those dear children to whom He
will say, "Come, ye blessed of my Father."

. . . Your own dear mother.

The "worth" of such a woman, speaking so naïvely
and justly to her own daughter, cannot be long in coming
home to us. Which reminds me to quote, at this point, the
remark made by Father Dufour d'Astafort, s.j., in an ar-
ticle on Madame De Barberey's *Elizabeth Seton, et les
commencements de l'Eglise Catholique aux États Unis*
(published in 1868): "A candid Protestant," he says,
". . . might indeed, at first thought, credit his church
with the virtues which Elizabeth practiced while a member of it; but . . . he will be obliged to acknowledge that
if many such persons as she have taken the road to Rome,
never has a Catholic of her worth passed over to Protestantism."

This passage was written when Protestantism
was an determined, if inadequate, force in the world of
Christian thought. In my own day, when the conflict
is not only between heresy and truth, but between truth
and utter darkness, some few souls will relish my talking

about the Christian realism of Elizabeth Seton, the realism of a strong soul shaped by God. That it was shaped by God, is my belief; and let me say confidently it is also the belief of the Sovereign Pontiff, Christ's Vicar, who has raised her to our altars, and thereby given her, in all her delightfulness, not only to the American people, but the whole Catholic world: *Urbi et Orbi.*

Spiritual Director

In all biography, I imagine, some interesting sidelights are discovered in connection with one's story. And I think it would be unfair to my readers not to tell this one, which amused me greatly.

One of the documents I have at hand is: *Memoir, Letters and Journal of Mrs. Seton,* edited by her grandson, Archbishop Robert Seton (published in 1870. In this work is printed a letter which Elizabeth penned describing the arrival of the plague-stricken Irish immigrants at the Quarantine in New York. Elizabeth had written, "The first thing these poor people did when they got their tents was to assemble on the grass and all kneeling adore their Maker for His mercy, and every morning's sun finds them repeating His praise." Archbishop Seton notes that when the letter (written to her sister-in-law, Rebecca) was returned to Elizabeth after Rebecca's death, Elizabeth crossed out the "their" before "Maker" and wrote "our" instead. Archbishop Seton handles the incident in the following footnote:

"The Protestant Episcopal Church is not a church of the people. It is a Church of the few, of the rich, of those whose refinement repugns association even in the House of God with ill-clad, coarse and lowly folks. Hence it becomes somewhat difficult for one of this denomination—especially if she be a dainty lady—to believe that there is one and the same Father in Heaven and on earth of her and of the lousy tatterdemalion who kneels in filth to adore."

Appended to this footnote is another in pencil, written by some previous owner of my volume, expunging the Archbishop's epithet "lousy." Rarely have I seen so much crossing-out done on a page, and by such a variety of persons.

In the bearing of her third child (Richard) both Elizabeth and her little son were at one time given up for dead. Nevertheless she went on to bear two more children, which is the way with all noble, happy people who consider motherhood a sacrifice and an honor. Also there were bad fever plagues in New York in those days, fevers of all different kinds (and there are so many kinds no one can count them; Typhoid, Scarlet, and Yellow were three of the especially virulent types). Naturally, in a soul so sensitive to love in all its forms, whether connubial, maternal, filial, or, in what the French call *amitié*, Elizabeth's spirit was harassed at the thought that disease in the shape of germs was always surrounding her children; and she was sympathetic enough to feel that if her child was fortuitously saved from the ravages of a plague, some other mother's child was not. The quality of her notes and letters during the first four years of her marriage may be rightly interpreted in terms of the alarm she had for the safeguard of her own little ones (for whose existence she could be somewhat "blamed") when she saw children dying around her in hundreds in that heroic, albeit unsanitary, age of the late seventeen-hundreds.

In June, 1798, the elder Seton, William, Sr., died.

Whether he had not as good a business head as he thought
he had, or whether the crash in his financial affairs was
bound to come anyhow through the failure of his ships
and his investments (and this was probably the case, because Seton père was much worried about his assets
just before his death), the fact of the matter was that
William Seton, Jr., and his saintly wife had many hardships to encounter from the fourth year of their marriage
until the younger William's death.

She was as equal to poverty as she was to wealth.
But he was not. He was a brooder. This was due in large
measure, no doubt, to the character of his disease. What
his disease was is not definitely known. It seems to have
been some sort of tubercular infection, for he coughed up
phlegm and blood, but Elizabeth testifies that it had also
attacked his intestines, and, as Dr. Weir Mitchell once
remarked, any disease lower than the diaphragm always
causes melancholy. Melancholy, in the Greek origin of the
word, means "black bile," and if you have it, there is no
way of being cheerful about it.

Though Elizabeth could say of her husband in writing to his sister, at the time of their great financial stress:
"Never did mortal sustain with such firmness and such
patience the strokes of adversity," and though in his final
distress he seems to have caught from her beautiful spirit
the courage to bear the most extreme suffering with fortitude and no complaint, yet in a letter to one of her friends,
Mrs. Julia Scott ("my dearest Juliana"), written in 1798,
I think she analyzes him most justly and objectively. She
says then of her husband: "His disposition is of that kind
which does not admit of the soothings of sympathy, but

wraps itself in the stillness of despair. This but little suits
the anxious solicitude of my cares for him." Yet in the
tender care of a bride who literally burned him up with
her own spiritual ardor and faith, to what heroisms the
soul of William Seton could attain in his last agony, we
shall see.

Their loss of fortune was moderately well sustained
by the Setons while Doctor Bayley lived, and for long
periods at a time Elizabeth and one or other or all of her
children went to live with him. But at his death in August
of 1801, despite her efforts to cheer herself up with
clichés and slogans, it seems life began to appear to her
quite insupportable. It was at this time that she undertook to receive spiritual direction at the hands of another.
Hitherto, her spiritual life had been the outgrowth of her
own ardent nature, her readings in the Scriptures and
elsewhere, and the constant impulse of Grace that was
making her seek, as far as she could find them in her ter-
ritory, the paths to Christian perfection.

The spiritual director achieved by her at this stage
was one Reverend Henry Hobart, assistant rector at
Trinity Church, New York, who on occasion was loaned
to grace the pulpits of Saint Paul's and Saint Mark's.
Afterwards he was to become a Bishop.

In his memoir of his grandmother, Archbishop
Robert Seton comes in contact with the Reverend Henry
Hobart. The moment he does so you can see the Archbishop drawing up into a sarcastic reserve, anxious to
fight it out in the rôle of a priest who has a sacrament of
Holy Orders to enable him to undertake the spiritual
guidance of souls, as against an evangelical who has not.

And that is undoubtedly why Elizabeth's sacerdotal grandson is hard on the Reverend Hobart. "Henry Hobart" says Archbishop Seton, "was a man, by manners and education, eminently fitted to captivate gentle spirits, and lead them whichever way he would. Elizabeth was, I may say, *infatuated* by this eloquent Reverend, and is another illustration that in a religious body whose clergy's title to consideration rests on personal merits alone, the devotion of some to their pastors is only equalled by the contempt of others."

It is machine-gun attack all the way between Elizabeth's own flesh-and-blood biographer and the Rev. Mr. Hobart. When she declares in a letter to Rebecca (August 16, 1802): "Our Henry Hobart was at St. Mark's instead of St. Paul's yesterday afternoon, and William told me that those who heard him said he was a great contrast to the gentleman *we* had, who had given in the morning a schism sermon. Surely H. H's knew nothing of schism. . . . William left me at the door and I sat half an hour before the bell had ceased ringing, then looking up I saw Henry Hobart in the pulpit. Such *fervent prayers* I never heard before: about *eight* to join . . ." Robert Seton comments acridly: "Verily a large congregation, and most gratifying to the man who rang the bell so long."

This is pretty strong fire. The sentence which struck me most in the above quotation was "Surely H.H's knew nothing of schism." I think this is a most touching and significant remark from one who would perforce call herself a Protestant if asked what she was at this juncture.

Likewise, in a later tribute when Elizabeth writes:

"Language cannot express the comfort, the hope, the peace which followed Hobart's words; but William did not understand. We went twice to church, my own William and I, and our two eldest, but only to hear strangers. It was good however, and we were well satisfied, but the superlative rests with Henry Hobart." Robert Seton, in retort, has ready this commentary: "Since Protestants have no Sacrifice, it is easily understood how every thing in their service practically hinges on the sermon. A good preacher will always be the idol of his congregation, and if a 'stranger' happens to take his place, the disappointment is very great."

Whatever be the merits of this battle, Mr. Hobart could hardly be blamed for being the possessor of handsomeness, eloquence and charm, and it was something to have dedicated these to some sort of service of God. And if he attained nothing else but the giving of a temporary peace to the soul of Elizabeth Seton at a moment when she greatly needed comfort, and when her William, "who did not understand," most needed support, it was something to have been born for this reason alone. And I am certain that as Elizabeth corresponded more and more exquisitely to grace, she was as generous in her forgiveness of the Reverend Mr. Hobart's heavy invectives as she had formerly been generous in her admiration of him when he enthralled her with his pulpit eloquence and "fervent prayers."

However, the retroactive anxiety of Robert Seton for his grandmother's soul at this period is also understandable. He knew, as we all must, that the borderline between "spiritual direction" and "spiritual possession" is sometimes very slight and hard to measure, especially so when one's Gospel is one's personal charm. It is our trust, as priests, that our sacrament of Holy Orders enables us to overcome this weakness whenever an especially beautiful soul is entrusted to our counsel. If it does not, because we have not measured up to the strength of our sacrament, then wherever we shall have directed another, we shall have directed ourselves toward eternal damnation.

Again, in the case of an exceptionally exquisite soul, unattainable in any gross sense because of its integrity and honor, there is often a tendency to dominate at least what one cannot possess. Everyone knows how the modern psychiatrist loves to drive innocence to cover in the admissions of moral weaknesses that will support his scientific theory. And if anything is surer than sure, it is that many a professor in a co-educational college (sometimes a wizened old sour puss at that) has been known to direct his lectures exclusively and undistractedly toward the intellectual dominance of the most virtuous girl in the class, an especially attractive target if he be an agnostic, and she a Catholic, a Child of Mary.

At any rate, it was in the latter part of 1801 that Elizabeth, in her own trusting, judicious, and chaste fashion, became, so to speak, Mr. Hobart's disciple. He had been mentioned in letters previous to this, and seems to have been Rebecca's discovery, not Elizabeth's. But on August 15, 1802, she was admitted under his direction to the sacrament of the Lord's Supper, "as they call it," adds Robert Seton. Of course it was never told her that the Lord's Supper, "as they call it," was

intended in its authentic form to be the substantial
presence, under the appearance of bread and wine, of
the Body, Blood, Soul, and Divinity of Our Lord, Jesus
Christ. The Episcopalian rite, elucidated to Elizabeth at
this time by the Reverend Hobart, called for nothing
more than a commemorative service, an eating of plain
bread and drinking of plain wine, with a certain metaphorical reference to what Christ ordained in the Supper
Room when he said "This is My Body and This is My
Blood." Yet in her sweet fashion of always having an instinct for the Christian realities, it is told of dear Elizabeth that after her first admission to this rite, she would
often want to go from church to church on Sunday to repeat this "communion" with her Lord, and would even
beg the sexton to give her the leavings, the dregs of the
"sacrament" that had been brought back to the sacristy
when the worship was over, and the lees were on the point
of being thrown to the pigeons outside the window.

Robert Seton summarizes the whole situation as
follows: "Indeed I do not find that she reached until com-
paratively late the standard of even Protestant piety, for
she became a religionist in the sober and delusive manner
of her respectable sect only in the year 1802." And he
adds that her reception of the Lord's Supper was "in
company with and probably induced by her sister-in-law,
Rebecca Seton."

Whether Robert Seton's choice of adjectives "sober
and delusive" are the right ones, he is certainly correct in
saying that after her "conversion" in 1802, her letters and
notes all take on an unwonted sober manner. Incapable of
giving her any real doctrine except the most evasive kind,

Mr. Hobart must overwhelm her with "morals," an un-
balanced Christian program which broods dreadfully
over a sensitive Christian soul, expectant to receive the
comforts of Revelation to compensate for its hardships
and asceticisms. In no time Henry Hobart had her admitting that so far she had led "a gay and rather worldly
life, and had let her youth go by without much *practical*
regard to the duties imposed by religion, or found in the
sacred pages of the Gospel." Could anything be more absurd in the face of what we know of a girl whose life
was an open book from the time of her birth to her death?
And what "a practical regard" to the duties imposed by
religion consisted in for the moment, other than to listen-
ing to Reverend Hobart's sermons, cannot be imagined.
Most likely he was not too pleased that she should have
wanted the Lord's Supper to be too literally a sacrament,
and probably "tut-tutted" the fact that she did not like
to see the verger throw the leavings away to the grass and
the birds. If she was the most precious of his worshipers,
I can also understand how she might have been the most
difficult.

The confidences entrusted by Elizabeth to her diary
at this period are altogether too informed with the "re-
vivalist" spirit, and altogether too shorn of the natural
cheerfulness and gaiety of her normal character. Such
entries as these will illustrate the reason for this affirma-
tion:

"Almighty and Giver of all mercies, Father of all, who
knows my heart and pities its weakness and errors: Thou
knowest the desire of my soul to do Thy will. It struggles
to wing its flight to Thee its creator and sinks again in

sorrow for that imperfection which draws it back to earth. How long shall I contend with sin and mortality."

"Redeemer of sinners! who gave Thy life to save us, assist a miserable sinner who strives with the corruption and desires above all things to break the snares of the enemy."

"The chosen ministering servant bids us to the feast." (Hobart.)

On the 20th of July, 1802, Elizabeth's last child was born, and named Rebecca, after the child's aunt. The rebound is not too characteristic. "Solemnly in the presence of my Judge I resolve to remember my infirmity and my sins—to keep the door of my lips—to consider the causes of sorrow for sin in myself and them whose souls are dear to me as my own; to check and restrain all useless words —to deny myself and exercise the severity that I know is due to my sins; to judge myself hereby trusting, through mercy, that I shall not be severely judged by my Lord."

This last is hardly the canticle of a young mother having safely delivered a beautiful baby-girl child.

Anyhow, on the 29th of September we find her writing again. "This day my little Rebecca is received into the Ark of Our Lord; she has been blessed by his chosen servant." It would seem, would it not, that the being received into the Ark of the Lord, was chiefly effected because of the welcome of "his chosen servant"? (Hobart again.)

But this period was not to go on for long. By what was a merciful dispensation of Divine Providence, it was arranged that Elizabeth should change the "sober and delusive" air of her present surroundings for the warm, rich,

Mr. and Mrs. William Seton
about the time of their marriage (1794)

From two miniatures by an unknown artist
Courtesy of the Sisters of Charity of Mount Saint Vincent

Mother Elizabeth Ann Seton

From a pastel by Enrique Dorda based on an authentic miniature
Courtesy of the Sisters of Charity of Mount Saint Vincent

Catholic life of Italy, in which two notable Christian gentlemen, with no pretensions at being "directors of souls," but in the modest rôle of honorable friends, should come to recognize the preciousness of this soul and give it, what it most craved at this moment, some doctrine instead of a steady diet of "uplift."

Please do not think that the Reverend Mr. Hobart of the charming eloquence and the fervent prayers was entirely a cloud in Elizabeth's career. He was only a mist, through which some light shone, but not enough. And it was too dismal for the needs of her sanctification.

In the course of the year 1803 (Elizabeth is now twenty-nine years of age, and the mother of five children) her husband William's health began to fail so seriously that he contemplated taking a voyage to Italy to visit his old friends, the Filicchis, in whose banking house he had served an apprenticeship as a boy. What wild delirium made him think of Italy at the moment no one can know, except as an interpretation of God's Providence, which was much more concerned with the sanctification of his wife than of himself, since she, not he, was the spiritual prize in this most happy union.

How anyone at this stage could have felt that Italy was more beneficial to a pulmonary and intestinal infection than fresh-aired America, is hard to understand. It may be that the doctors felt the sea voyage would at least be advantageous. At any rate, William Seton, in the throes of his lung-bleeding and dysentery, kept clamoring for Italy as a place of respite, if not of repair. He had some money left; not much, despite his intense application to the business interests his father had left him. But it might be better to attempt to revive a wrecked constitution at the moment, in the hope of restoring a wrecked fortune later. Our physical ills seem somehow always to get in the way of our financial.

Elizabeth's indoctrination by the Reverend Henry Hobart was not distasteful to William Seton. He must have noticed the soberization of his wife's once exuberant spirits. But he was as generous as she in paying compliments to Hobart, and was, as we have seen, in the habit of taking her to church in order to let her hear him preach. It ought also in justice to be admitted that two or three things the Reverend Hobart said touched the soul of William acutely and he confessed—to her delight—that he was much impressed.

Yet there was always an uninterpreted nostalgia in his soul for the company of those exemplary Italian gentlemen in whose household he had spent the happy days of his youth. "The Filicchis!" he kept saying to himself. "Much of what Henry Hobart says I do not understand, despite the fact that my beautiful wife does." But there was in the Filicchis something one did not need to understand in the discursive sense. One got it by atmosphere, by instinct. And so, absurd as it seems, William, in a state fit to take not even a carriage ride, demanded that he go to Italy, to live again with Antonio and Filippo Filicchi and see there if he could not overcome his nauseas and dysenteries.

His wife determined to accompany him. She knew, much as she might hate to admit it, that of all her children, William was unquestionably her baby. They had

means enough to take only one child with them: Anna
Maria, the oldest. The other four children would have to
be left with friends, friends who are always strangers as
far as children are concerned. How was Elizabeth to
know that on this excursion William would die? She
could not know it, but it is my belief that Grace knew it
for her. Thus it was that, in the face of all that was imprudent, Elizabeth booked a passage on the brig *The
Shepherdess,* a small commercial ship that was soon to set
sail (literally) from New York to the shores of Italy.

The Reverend Henry Hobart had, of course, to be
notified of this project. And it is at this point where we
all must agree with Elizabeth's to-be priest-grandson and
find Hobart most unsatisfactory. He knew he was losing
a prize. He makes a desperate effort to attach a lien to
her in the following departure letter.

"My heart bleeds for you, my valued friend. I feel
the impotence of language to console you, and in this
pressing exigency I rejoice that an Almighty Creator is at
hand. . . . Go then, my afflicted friend; my deep sympathy, my feeble ardent blessing goes with you. With the
fervent solicitude of your pastor, your friend, your
brother, my soul will not cease to implore for you and
yours, the protecting presence, the consoling grace of
your Redeemer and God."

This is obviously sincere and straightforward, however heavy. But soon follows the significant admonition:

"I miss you and the family at church, but wherever
you are God will hear and receive your prayer. The
sumptuous and splendid worship of Italy will not, I am

sure, withdraw your affections from the simple but affecting worship of Trinity Church. . . ."

Alas, poor Henry Hobart! He seems to sense at this
moment that the most precious fish ever caught in his net
was soon to wriggle out of it. That he was to become
nasty after her conversion to the True Faith is to be expected. And for that we almost excuse him. There is no
fun in instructing a "convert," especially when the conversion is away from what you intended. Thousands of An-
glican (Episcopalian) ministers have discovered that in
the last two centuries. This may be the reason, partly,
why one thousand of them since Newman's time have followed their catechumens into the Catholic Church, for
which entrance they supplied the necessary preliminary
instruction, and only fell short when what they proclaimed to be "Catholic" was demanded in fact to be
Catholic by the fortunate devotees of their "almost"
Christian Revelation.

And so William's demands for a sea voyage and
a visit to the Filicchis in Italy were acceded to, and, after
a careful scrutiny as to what the personnel of the trip
should be, Elizabeth decided to leave four of her children
with relatives and friends in New York; and in the company of her all but collapsed husband and their eldest
child, Anna Maria (aged eight), she took passage on
October 2, 1803, from New York to Leghorn.

All their friends were at the boat. There was much
affectionate embracing (for they were a well-loved cou-
ple), much waving of handkerchiefs, a considerable
amount of tears, and, finally, a fond farewell, as the little

brig *The Shepherdess,* under command of Captain (and Mrs.) O'Brien put out full sail, and they left New York for the long voyage to the land God made "when He was gay and young."

Inasmuch as this departure marks a definite change in Elizabeth's life and destiny, I think we should conclude this chapter with some of the excerpts found in her diary and letters, to indicate the quality of her soul at this period and its thereabouts. Neglecting for the moment the discouraged spiritual notes written during the Hobart influence, we find her to have said in these happy, though arduous, days of her early married life about as many charming things as any wife would be expected to say in any situation like hers. Here are a few of the precious things she revealed of herself in her writings:

To her Father: I have passed one of the quietest evenings in my life. It is now eleven o'clock, and I have been sitting here since seven. I have been reading of the "High and lofty One who inhabits Eternity," and selecting such passages as I wish to let my daughter see. How the world lessens and recedes! How calm and peaceable are hours spent in such solitude! They are marked down for useful purposes and their memory remains. I close my evening employment with orisons for thee. Peace be with father.

To Julia Scott: Think, Julia, how many we have outlived whose lives we calculated upon as certain to be of longer duration than our own! and how unable we are to judge of future events! If your fear is realized, remember the never-failing Protector we have. But He will not divide your confidence; rely solely on Him, and from experience I can declare that it will produce the most peaceful sensations and most perfect enjoyments of which the heart is capable.

To Rebecca Seton: I have often told you, my Rebecca, that I had determined never again to allow myself the enjoyment of any affection beyond the bounds of moderation, but, really, your loving letters, the remembrance of past hours, and the thousand thoughts of you that strike me every day at this place, make it no easy matter to restrain my expressions when I write to you. I never dust about the house, or dress the flower-pots, or walk in the garden, but it seems you are as much my companion as if you were actually near us; and last evening finding myself by the garden wall at the spot whereon we used to stand at sunset last fall, anticipating in our pleasant talk what we would do this summer, I was so struck by the recollection and the uncertainty of when I should see you again, that I had a hearty crying spell, which is not a very common thing with me, nor do I suppose would have happened but that I have ever since the first moment you left me had a strong presentiment that our separation was for a long while.

To Lady Cayley: I think, my dear aunt, that I have given you a pretty good account of us all, except my own three sweet children who I can *reasonably* assure you are not surpassed by any. My Anna Maria is the very model of all we could even wish for her; and perhaps my change of life [her father-in-law's death] may be one of her greatest advantages, as it has altered her young mother into an old one, better calculated to watch the progress of her active little mind. William grows so wonderfully like his grandfather, that you would scarcely believe it possible a child could be so much like a parent; and appears to have as many traces of his disposition and manners as he has of his features. Richard, our youngest [at that time], is, if possible, lovelier than either. I am his nurse, as I have been to all the others, and although he is able to stand up and lay his head upon my bosom, I can find no courage to wean him yet.

To her Husband: Your letter, dearest William, which I received last evening, made me lively and happy as a bird. That you pass your time well and are in good health and spirits gave me inexpressible pleasure. It makes me feel selfish in wishing your return.

To herself: After six hours of undisturbed sleep, when the stars were disappearing before the light my soul awoke. The body also sweetly refreshed left it at liberty to adore and to renew its devotion to the Creator, Redeemer, and Sanctifier; all my little flock were resting peaceably within the fold. Well might their mother arise to acknowledge, to praise, and to bless the gracious Shepherd who preserves them safe in His refuge, feeds them with His hand, and leads them to the refreshing stream, well may she follow on, confiding them to His care, rejoicing in His presence, triumphing in His protection, and seeking only to express her grateful joy and love: seeking His favor but by submission to His will. O Lord, keep us in Thy way, direct us in Thy paths, recall our wanderings, make us to hear Thy voice with gladness and to rejoice in Thy salvation.

Was there ever such a versatile and exquisite soul in our land, on our shores?

It was such a lady that the Providence of God entrusted to the sail-boat of Captain O'Brien, with her daughter and ailing husband, on October 3, 1803, in their

valiant attempt (they were the only passengers) to cross
the Atlantic Ocean in an indefinite search for health and
peace in Italy. The ship was named *The Shepherdess*.

And incidentally, there was a reality in the Christian
Revelation of which neither Elizabeth's books, nor her
father, nor her Henry Hobart had ever made the slightest mention, of which not one single word ever crops up
in her letters from the day of her birth till the hour of
this voyage to Europe. This reality is the Woman who
is perhaps the peculiar secret of Catholics, though why,
God knows, since she is emblazoned mightily in the
prophecies of the Old Testament and the fulfilments of
the New. And her name might not be inappropriately
called "The Shepherdess." And of her much will be
learned in Italy, one of her favorite lands, among the race
that calls her "Madonna Mía."

The Shepherdess

A man terribly interested in navigation (or maybe just terribly interested in queer stunts) recently threw five hundred bottles into the Atlantic Ocean at some point on the Continent, and he found it was possible for one of them to float to the shores of the United States in a period of seven months.

The little *Shepherdess* was almost four times as fast as that bottle. It crossed from New York to Leghorn in fifty-six days. In that number of days modern transatlantics could cross a dozen times.

Captain and Mrs. O'Brien were, as may have been suspected by the reader, Irish. The Irish in many situations are difficult people. But I can imagine no more delightful companions on a long sea voyage, especially in the dark nights when there was only a lantern shining to identify them on the great ocean underneath the stars, than a jovial Irishman, full of stories, punctuating all his dramatic tales with devoirs to "the love of God," "the grace of God," "the Mother of God," etc., and his exuberantly sympathetic and solicitous Irish wife (who had on board an eighteen-months' old daughter). It is easy to surmise what tenderness and care they must have lavished on such a genteel lady as Elizabeth, such a poor sick husband as William, and such a darling child as Anna Maria.

The Setons and the O'Briens got along famously, as Elizabeth testifies. In fact, they got along intimately, so intimately that Anna Maria caught the whooping cough from the O'Brien child. I have heard that in the whooping cough it takes two weeks for the whoop to come, two weeks for it to stay, and two weeks for it to go. So it can be seen that poor little Anna Maria practically whooped her way all across the Atlantic.

Henry Seton, William's brother, accompanied them on the get-away from New York harbor, left them the next day as a pick-up on a returning boat, and brought back from Elizabeth two brief notes to Rebecca as the first fruits of her trip:

12 o'clock, off the Light-House
October 2d, 1803

My soul's Sister—Our William felt the passing of the Battery so much that I scarcely could wave my handkerchief. But since that he has been very composed and better than on shore. My heart is uplifted and feels its treasure, and the little Book and my cross are sources of peace and sweet comfort. He is with me, what can I fear? Your being sick is the greatest care I leave behind me, but that too must be referred to our All-sufficient. My friend and brother's [Hobart's] deserted dwelling started my first tear—the study windows were all I could see.

10 o clock, Oct. 3d

Henry is leaving us, all goes well. The Lord on high is mightiest. A storm threatens, but I fear not with Him. Bless my darling girls [Harriet and Cecilia Seton], and kisses to my little ones.

And so with much experience of being with wind and without it, by veering, tacking, maneuvering, putting up

one kind of sail and then another, after desperate buffet-
ings in the night of the high waves of storm, after having
been boomed over by thunder and flashed upon by lightning, and after much lazy lolling in the dead calms and
in the hot sun, and after having managed not to be
sighted by the pirates of Barbary, who were prowling in
the waters near her course, *The Shepherdess,* decidedly
outdistancing any floating bottles that happened to be following, managed on the twenty-fifth day of her voyage to
reach what Elizabeth would call "the Western Islands"
and we "the Azores," just half way between New York
and Leghorn. . . . Nearly two weeks later they were in
Gibraltar Bay.

"In Gibraltar Bay!" Elizabeth exclaims in her diary,
and then goes on to tell herself of a dream she had while
the wind blew through the sails one lonely night and all
the three Setons, including Elizabeth, were asleep.

"Was climbing" she says "with great difficulty a
mountain of immense height and blackness, and when
near the top, almost exhausted a voice said—'Never
mind, take courage, there is a beautiful green hill on the
other side, and on it an angel waits for you.'" To those
of you who think that no dreams should be believed in,
and do not know how to separate the real ones from the
nightmares, this dream will mean nothing. Yet it was
strangely fulfilled.

It was only a short while after this that Reverend
Henry Hobart was writing to her from America: "My
heart has accompanied you across the ocean. I have felt
its boisterous storms. My prayers have ascended to
heaven for your safety." We might almost suspect, there-

fore, that he was the "angel" in the dream. But no. The
dream distinctly said the angel was on a beautiful green
hill "on the other side." So he was not the angel. Nor
will he probably want to be called the "mountain," especially since I had occasion to call him "a mist" a few
pages back.

The dream must really have haunted Elizabeth, for
a week later we find her writing in her diary one of the
most beautiful renunciatory prayers of her life. It is a
bewildered prayer, but awe-fully beautiful. While William dozed and coughed under his blanket and little Anna
Maria turned feverishly in her sleep, Elizabeth wrote:
"14th November.—Considering the infirmity of corrupt
nature which would overpower the spirit of grace, and
the enormity of the offence to which the least indulgence
of them would lead me, in the anguish of my soul shud-
dering to offend my adored Lord, I have this day solemnly engaged that through the strength of His holy
spirit I will not again expose that corrupt and infirm nature to the smallest temptation I can avoid; and if my
Heavenly Father will once more re-unite us, that I will
make a daily sacrifice of every wish, even the most innocent, lest they should betray me to a deviation from the
solemn vow I have now made. O my God! imprint it on
my soul with the strength of Thy Holy Spirit, that by His
grace, supported and defended, I may never more forget
that Thou art *my all*, and that I can not be received in
Thy heavenly kingdom without a pure and faithful heart,
supremely devoted to Thy holy will. Oh, keep me for the
sake of Jesus Christ."

Still the boat sailed on, and no land as yet. Two

nights later there was another storm. And again Elizabeth:

"16th November. A heavy storm of rain with thunder and lightning at midnight. . . . After reading a great deal, and long and earnest prayer, went to bed again but could not rest. A little voice (my own Anna's who I thought was asleep), in a soft whisper said: 'Come hither, all ye weary souls.' I changed my place to her arms, the rocking of the vessel and breaking of the waves were forgotten, the heavy sighs and restless pains were lost in sweet refreshing sleep. Adored Redeemer, it was Thy word by the voice of one of Thy little ones, who promises indeed to be one of Thy angels."

Two days later, just at sundown, on the eighteenth of November, 1803, while the Ave Maria bells were ringing in the village, while the peasant boy knelt in prayer in the middle of the road, and the housewife crossed herself in her doorway, just when the old banana seller took off his hat and raised his eyes toward the Immaculate Lady of the Incarnation, and even the village donkey stopped his trotting to join in the holy silence, *The Shepherdess* brought Elizabeth of New York into the port of Leghorn.

The Lazaretto

But no. There was to be no Leghorn for them for many a long day yet.

There is no purified soul without a purification, just as there is no brave soul without an endangerment, no humble soul without humiliation. "Not this, not this, not this, not this is your end, your goal," says God about all the good things of this earth, "but Myself." Of course, if there were no God, this were an impossible, tragic régime. But if He *is,* and (in the true sense in which it can be taken) if there is *nothing* but Him, what wonder that He should disappoint us, endanger us, humiliate us, even frighten us into His own arms!

Elizabeth had rightly supposed that after the interminable voyage from the harbor of New York to that of Leghorn, it might well be within the designs of the Providence of God to allow her now a respite. The admirable Filicchis were waiting to extend to her and hers the full extent of their hospitality. What is more, her half-brother Carlton was living in Leghorn, having been taken into the counting-house of the Filicchis because he was William's half-brother-in-law.

Carlton had prepared a reception for them at the dock. He even had a band, rehearsed them, even taught them the "Hail Columbia," and, as Elizabeth remarks in her journal, "all those little tunes that set the darlings dancing at home." Never was such a welcome to have been given to weary voyagers when they first set foot on

Italian soil. William, so sick and tired of his uncomfortable mattress and the jogging and swaying of the boat, was ready to burst into tears. Little Anna Maria was dancing on the deck in anticipation of all the joy that had been promised her. Elizabeth herself, in the face of the delights to come, had to hide herself in her berth to weep of very joy. Everything was ready for a riot of rejoicing at their debarkment.

Elizabeth says, "When I heard in the morning a boat was alongside of our ship, I flew on deck and would have thrown myself in the arms of dear Carlton; but he retired from me, and a guard, whom I saw for the first time, said, 'Don't touch!'"

Why "Don't touch"?

Here's why. The *Shepherdess* was the first to bring news from New York of the plague of yellow fever which had broken out there. The Setons had no yellow fever, but the boat lacked a bill of health to show that they hadn't; or at least hadn't germs still clinging to them that would give the yellow fever to others. And the Italian authorities were enough acquainted with the problem of germs in those days, little as they knew about serums and antiseptics to counteract them, to be wary about accepting as immigrants three possibly germ-laden individuals from America, however graciously they might have been willing to accept them under other circumstances.

Well, what was to be done? There were rules for such emergencies. They were to be taken to a pest-house, some miles up the bay, called, not "a hospital for infectious diseases," but by the ironically picturesque name of "a Lazaretto." The word derives obviously from Laz-

arus the leper, who had perforce to go about in Our
Lord's time crying "Unclean! Unclean!"

No landing for the poor Setons at Leghorn. They
could wave to their friends, Carlton and the Filicchis
standing on the pier. But "Don't touch" was soon sup-
plemented with the order "Don't land." And they didn't.

Instead there appeared a boat rowed by fourteen
oars; a smaller boat was fastened to it in which the Setons were placed, being allowed a minimum of baggage
and only one change of clothes; and they were rowed to
the Lazaretto, situated some miles out of the town of
Leghorn.

The journey took about an hour. The bells were
tolled, signifying that some pest-ridden inmates were arriving; the chains across the canal that guarded the establishment from the ingress of indiscriminate boats were let
down; the sailors on shore and on deck began shouting
and quarreling as to the precise point at which these out-
casts should be allowed to disembark; the Monsieur le
Capitano, who had charge of the Lazaretto, arrived and
did much whispering and consulting as to how these suspect passengers were to be maneuvered and disposed of;
and then, at the point of a bayonet, which presumably
could not at a distance incur any infection, William Seton
(just about able to totter), his wife Elizabeth, and their
daughter, Anna Maria, arrived for their first taste of
Italy.

Captain O'Brien of *The Shepherdess* had ready a
letter of instructions to offer to Monsieur le Capitano
of the Lazaretto, some of them informative, others
pleading. These were accepted on the point of a stick,

read, and the letter immediately burned. Elizabeth insisted on taking some books and papers. They were carefully examined (as if for germs). The mattresses and the
small baggage allowed the Setons were likewise carefully
examined. The inspector was a man who had, we may say
the least, an unmicroscopic pair of eyes, but who was condemned, because of this function, to serve a sentence of
quarantine in the Lazaretto as long as the Setons themselves. It can hardly have escaped the minds of William,
Elizabeth, and Anna Seton, that they had taken this long,
hard voyage to Italy for the sake of "health." Anna
trembled in fright, William Seton staggered out of the
boat as if at any moment he might collapse, and amidst
many attempted commiserations on the part of the Capitano, whose heart was not in his work as a gaoler, William was carried into the Lazaretto, while behind him
walked sadly his wife and child. It was the day of November 19, 1803.

What follows is told by Elizabeth herself in one of
the most revealing documents ever penned. Some of the
soul travails of the saints can be guessed at, but Elizabeth
has set down in her "Journal" a detailed account of her
detention in this pest-house of Italy, and with such pathos,
such intimacy, such innocence, and (may I add) such
brilliance, that I should only defeat the purpose of my
story at this point if I did not let her tell some of it for
herself. We shall begin with the account that is dated:

19th Nov. 10 o'clock at night.... We were directed
to go opposite the Capitano's house, in which sat Mrs.
Phillip Filicchi, compliments and kind looks without num-

ber. A fence was between us, but I fear did not hide my
fatigue of soul and body. We had chairs handed us, which
after we had touched could not go back to the house. At
length we were shown the door we should enter, No. 6,
up twenty steps. A room with high arched ceiling like St.
Paul's, brick floor, whitewashed walls, and a jug of water.
The Capitano sent three warm eggs, a bottle of wine, and
some slips of bread. William's mattress was soon spread
and he upon it. I then found there was a little recess in
which my knees found rest, and after emptying my heart,
and washing the bricks with my tears returned to my poor
William, and found him and Anna both in want of a
preacher. Dear child, she soon found a rope that had tied
her box and began jumping away to warm herself, for the
coldness of the bricks and walls made us shiver. At sunset dinner came from Mr. Filicchi with other necessaries;
we went again to the gate to see them.

My William and Anna are now sound asleep, and I
trust that God who has given them strength to go through
such a day of exertion will carry us on. *He* is our all indeed. My eyes smart so much with crying, wind, and
fatigue that I must close them and lift up my heart. Sleep
won't come very easily. If you had seen little Anna's arms
clasped around my neck at her prayers, while the tears
rolled a stream, how you would love her. I read her to
sleep with little pieces of trust in God. He is with us, and
if suffering abound in us, His consolations also greatly
abound, and far exceed all utterance. If the wind, for it
is said there was never such storms before at this season,
that now almost puts out my light and blows on my William through every crevice and down our chimney like loud
thunder, could come from any but His command, or if
the circumstances that have placed us in so forlorn a situ-

ation were not guided by His hand, miserable indeed would be our case. Within this hour William has had a violent fit of coughing, so as to bring up blood, which agitates and distresses him through all his endeavors to hide it. What shall we say? This is the hour of trial. The Lord support and strengthen us in it; retrospections bring anguish; press forward to the mark and prizes.

The strong counsel of her father can be seen in the last few sentences, but what a most vivid faith in God can be seen in the rest of it? William's perfect silence in the discourse of this narration is arresting. And watch closely little Anna, for if Elizabeth was an American Woman, she was an American Angel, indeed, it seems, the quintessence of the beauty of her mother's soul.

20th Nov. Sunday Morning. . . . The matin bells awakened my soul to its most painful regret and filled it with an agony of sorrow, which could not at first find relief even in prayer. In the little recess from whence there is a view of the open sea, and the beating of the waves against the high rocks at the entrance of the prison, which throw them violently back and raise the spray as high as its walls, I first came to my senses and reflected that I was offending my only Friend and resource in my misery, and voluntarily shutting out from my soul the only consolation it could receive. Pleading for mercy and strength brought peace and, with a cheerful countenance, I asked William what we should do for breakfast. The doors were opened and a bottle of milk set down in the middle of the room, Anna and William ate it with bread, and I walked the floor with a crust and a glass of wine. William could not sit up; his ague came on and my soul's

agony with it. My husband on the cold bricks without
fire, shivering and groaning, lifting his dim and sorrowful
eyes with a fixed gaze in my face while his tears ran on his
pillow without one word. Anna rubbed one hand and I
the other until his fever came on. The Capitano brought
us news that our time was lessened five days, told me to
be satisfied with the dispensations of God, etc., and was
answered by such a succession of sobs that he soon departed. Mr. Filicchi now came to comfort my William,
and when he went away he said as much of our blessed
service as he could go through; I then was obliged to lay
my head down. Dinner was sent and a servant to stay with
us during our quarantine. *Luigi,* a very little old man
with gray hair, and blue eyes that changed their expression from joy to sorrow as if they would console and still
enliven. My face was covered with a handkerchief when
he came in, and tired with the sight of men with military
hats, cockades, and bayonets I did not look up. Poor
Luigi! long shall I remember his voice of sorrow and tenderness when, at my refusing to eat, he looked up with
lifted hands in some prayer, that God would comfort me,
and I was comforted when I did not look at my poor
William, but to see him as he then lay was worse than to
see him dead. Now the bolts of another door are ham-
mered open, and Luigi (who had become an object of
equal terror with ourselves—having touched what we
had touched) had an apartment allotted to him. How
many times did the poor old man run up and down the
twenty nearly perpendicular steps to get things necessary
for our comfort for the next morning! When all was done
I handed him a chair that he might rest; he jumped almost
over it and danced around me like a madman, declaring he
would work all night to serve us. My William wearied out
was soon asleep, Anna with many tears prayed a blessing

and forgot her sorrow, and it seemed as if opening my prayer-book and bending my knees was the signal for my soul to find rest. It was nine o'clock with us and three at home; I imagined what I had often enjoyed and consoled myself with, the thought that though separated in the body six thousand miles, my soul and the souls I love were at the throne of grace at the same time, in the same prayers to our Almighty Father, accepted through our dear Redeemer and enlightened by our Blessed Spirit. Then did I rejoice indeed in the Lord, and triumph in the God of my salvation. After prayers read my little book of Sermons on Death, and became far more happy than I had been wretched. Went to bed at twelve, got up twice to pray and to help my dear William.

Luigi was undoubtedly the gift of the Filicchi brothers, and one can imagine with amazement and admiration the order proposed to him: would he mind going into a pest-house to attend to the wants of their dear friends, knowing that he must stay there, once in, until the time of their release? He did not mind, and went, with all his simple, clumsy courtesy (the very best kind in such a trial, because he was amusing as well as serviceable), and proved to be an excellent distraction.

Monday, 21st November.—Awoke with the same peace and comfort with which I had lain down, gave my William his physic and began to consider our situation, though so unfavorable to his complaint, as one of the steps in the dispensation of that Almighty will which alone could choose aught for us, and therefore set Anna to work and myself at the dear Scriptures as usual. Our Capitano came with his guards and put up a very neat bed and cur-

tains, sent by Mr. Filicchi, and fixed the benches upon
which Anna and I were to sleep; took down our names,
Signor Guglielmo, Signora Elizabeth, and *Signorina Anna
Maria.* The voice of kindness which again entreated
me to look up to the *bon Dieu* made me look up at the
speaker, and in our Capitano I found every expression of
a benevolent heart. His great cocked-hat being off, I saw
he had gray hairs, and a kind, affectionate countenance—
"I had a wife, I loved her, she gave me a daughter whom
she commended to my care—and died." He clasped his
hands, looked up, and then at my William. "If God calls,
what can we do, *et que voulez-vous, Signora?*"

I began to like my Capitano. Read and jumped the
rope to warm myself; looked round our prison and found
our situation was beautiful; comforted my William all I
could, rubbed his hands, wiped his tears, and gave words
to his soul, which was too weak to pray for itself. Heard
Anna read while I watched the sun setting in a cloud; after
both were asleep, read and prayed again till eleven. At
no loss to know the hour night and day, four bells strike
every hour and ring every quarter.

Elizabeth had, evidently, some Italian, and William
must have had plenty. But the strange mixture of French
and Italian (*Le Capitano,* and *que voulez vous, Signora*)
would seem to indicate that several languages were kept
flying in room Number 6 of the Lazaretto. Luigi probably got along better with them by actions and gesticula-
tions, than by words, as is indicated in the next entry.

Tuesday, 22d November.—My William was better
and very much encouraged by his Doctor Tutilli, who was
full of attention to him, also our Capitano, who now

seemed to understand me better. Talked with the Filicchis at the grate, and with great difficulty got my William up the steps again; read to him; heard Anna her lesson; and made the best of our situation. Our Luigi brought us an elegant bouquet of jasmines, geraniums, pinks, etc. No sun, heavy gales, which, if anything could move our walls, would certainly bring them down. The roaring of the sea sounds like thunder. Passed my evening as the last, quite reconciled to the sentinel, the bolts, bars, not afraid either of my candle, as the window shutter is almost the only piece of wood about us.

Elizabeth had indeed an ardent spirit, so generous, impulsive, and so gently possessive of everything that could inspire confidence, as is the way of the pure in heart. Notice the use in the above of "my William," "his Doctor Tutilli," "our Capitano," "our Luigi." Blessed are the pure of heart, for only they can talk affectionately, as only they can suffer pain.

Wednesday, 23d November.—Not only willing to take my cross but to kiss it too, and while glorying in our consolation, my poor William was taken with an ague which was almost too much; he told me (as he had often before) that it was too late, his strength was going from him every hour, and he would sink gradually, but it would not be long before he was gone. This to *me;* to his *friends* he was quite cheerful; as he was not able to go to them, they were admitted to the door, but must not touch the least thing; a wave of our Capitano's stick warned my William off, when in earnest conversation he would approach too near. A quiet half an hour at sunset and Anna and I sang our Advent hymns in a low voice. She said, while we were looking at the setting sun: "Mama, I dreamed last night that two persons had laid hold of me to kill me, and as one had struck my breast with a knife, in that instant I awoke, and found myself safe; and was thinking, so it will be with my *soul*—while I am struggling with death, in an instant I awake, and find myself safe from all that I feared, but *then:* forever." Our Jesus! After both were asleep, said our dear service alone. William had not been able in the day. Found Heavenly consolation. Forgot prison bolts and sorrow, and would have rejoiced to have sung with Paul and Silas.

Elizabeth never imagined as she wrote these precious documents in anguish and pathos, in a dark dungeon by the booming sea, by candlelight and with a scratchy pen, when her spirit was alone, standing on its mettle before no one but God, that well over a century later her fellow countrymen would be reading them to their delight and amazement.

The inescapable power she possessed and was to possess from now till her death was able to communicate her holiness to those around her, sanctifying her husband far beyond his temperament, and transmitting to her eight-year-old daughter a wisdom far beyond her years. There are times when one does not know who is the protagonist of spiritual greatness in this siege in the Lazaretto. Elizabeth was undoubtedly the soul of the three. But William was so sick, and Anna Maria so young! And yet from neither a word of complaint.

On the voyage over, in the midst of her racking cough and fever and pains, little Anna once moaned and then burst into tears, asking her mother to assure her that

God would not be displeased at her giving way to a sign
of complaint against what He was asking her to bear for
love of Him. There is a way in which this whole book
could be made into Anna Maria's story, just as it could
be made into William's, or even Rebecca's, Elizabeth's
soul's sister, for whom the journal recounted in this chapter was written. But we had better stick to the leading
character with which we started. For her triumph is, in
a sense, the triumph of them all. They were part of her,
her life: "My William—my Anna—my Rebecca. . . ."

It is now the 24th of November, 1803, and we have
spent exactly five days with Elizabeth in the dungeon of
Leghorn. William was constantly expressing the hope
that soon they would be released. Is twenty-five days
"soon"? If not, then we can have known how hopeless
were his hopes.

Night and day a sentinel with a gun paced up and
down outside the barred window. Why a sentinel armed?
Was not the kind, persuasive Capitano a sufficient police
force? It seems not. There were orders requiring the
sentry. And sometimes need of him. It could not always
be expected that the inmates of the Lazaretto would be as
gentle and controllable as the present incumbents of
Apartment 6.

"In this room," said the Capitano to Elizabeth,
"what sufferings have I seen! *There* lay an Armenian
begging a knife to end the struggles of death; *there* again,
where the *Signora's* couch is, a Frenchman, in the frenzy
of fever, insisted on shooting himself and died in ag-
onies."

There were billets of paper pasted above the door

to mark how many days different persons had stayed
there, marks on the wall and on the shutter: 10, 20, 30,
40 days. "I do not note ours," remarks Elizabeth,
"trusting they are numbered above."

Yet, with all her patience, she too could have her
own beautiful equivalent for rage, as when she writes:
"Ah! well I know that God is above, Capitano. You need
not give your silent look and point your finger always
there. If I thought our condition the providence of *man*,
you would find me willing to tear down your Lazaretto,
if it were possible that I might carry off my poor prisoner
to breathe the air of heaven in some seasonable place!"

And later this poignant passage in its combined
strength and weakness: "Here my husband, who left his
all to seek a milder climate, is confined in this high place
and within these damp walls, exposed to the cold and to
the dreary winds that penetrate to the very bones; without fire except the charcoal which oppresses his breast
so as nearly to convulse him; no little sirups, nor soother
of his cough; bark, warm milk, and opium pills (which he
takes quietly as a duty, without seeming to hope) is all I
can offer him from day to day. When nature fails, and I
can no longer look up with cheerfulness, I hide my face
in my hands on the chair by his bedside, and he thinks I
am praying; and pray I do, for prayer is all my comfort;
without it I should be of little service to him. Night and
day he calls me his life, his soul, his dearest of women, his
all."

More Lazaretto

Though sorrow still affecting ills prepares
   And o'er each passing day her presence lowers,
And darkened fancy shades with many cares,
   With many trials crowds the future hours
Still in the Lord will I rejoice,
Still to the Lord I lift my voice,
Father of mercies! still my grateful lays
Shall hymn Thy name, exulting in Thy praise.

> *(Poem by the Reverend J. H. Hobart, of which
> there are four other stanzas of identical tenor
> and theme, transcribed by Elizabeth Ann Seton
> in her Journal written in the Lazaretto of Leg-
> horn)*

And so, if we may imagine an invisible
hand, tearing off pages from a calendar (as is done in
the movies) until the number 30 has been arrived at, we
may follow Elizabeth's faithful account of herself in the
Lazaretto, barring only one week (that between December 5 and December 12), when there are no entries.

At one stage a gang of Turks, Greeks, Spaniards,
and Frenchmen were brought in, rescued from a ship-
wreck, and quartered in the room next to the Setons.
"No mattresses," says Elizabeth, "dry clothes, or food,
but all sent to one room, with naked walls, and the jug
of water, until the commandant shall find leisure to supply them."

81

Their racket, rage, and profanity in the next room brought this precious bit from Anna Maria. "For all we are so cold, and in this prison, mama, how happy we are compared with them; and we have peace, but they quarrel, fight, and cry out all the time." Bravest little lady, unbelievably understanding and courageous, who was to give even William a laugh one day, later, when she was reading from the Scriptures how John the Baptist was imprisoned!

"Yes, papa, Herod imprisoned him, but Miss Herodias gave him his liberty."

"No, dear, she had him beheaded."

"Ah! well papa, but she released him from prison by sending him to God."

"Child after my own heart," adds Elizabeth, commenting on this.

Captain and Mrs. O'Brien called, and both burst into tears at seeing William and Anna behind the grate. The mate from *The Shepherdess,* "who seems," says Elizabeth, "to love us as his own soul," also came. And Charles, one of the sailors.

"Why, Mrs. Seton," exclaimed Charles, "are you in prison?" And as he slowly retreated under orders, "shook his hand at Anna as long as he could see her." Whereupon Elizabeth adds: "How gracious is my adored Master, who gives even the countenances of strangers the look of kindness and pity."

One of the guards stationed to keep them in bounds, seeing the quality of her sympathy, sued for it. He put down his gun for a moment, and making pitiful gestures to his throat and chest, showed Elizabeth that he was sick. Elizabeth, touched, told the Capitano. Tut, tut! The Capitano would allow no sympathy for *him*. "Signora, he is very well off, has been married these two years to a handsome girl of sixteen, has two children, and receives three-and-sixpence a day."

There were humdrum days when the Journal has nothing to offer but "A storm of wind and very cold— Anna jumps the rope—Sung hymns and read to my William."

Every night, thinking of her children at home, were sent "two little white gulls flying to the westward towards my home, towards my loves." And these little white gulls were her two favorite prayers: the "We Praise Thee, O God," and the "Our Father."

There were kind remembrances too for Reverend J. H. H., thinking that he would say: "Poor soul, she will lose her reason in that prison." In gratitude for which sympathy she thought to thank him by conversing "with his angel."

There was also delirium, that kind that comes from such extreme fatigue that the body falls into a state of almost pleasant numbness, setting the imagination free to revel in some half-forgotten remembrance. In that remembrance, an event that happened long ago is brought back into existence with almost the same vividness it had when it occurred.

In the dead, still hour of noon, December 1, Elizabeth, wearied with the toil of constant administration to her husband, sat down, rested her head on the table, closed her eyes, and relived again one of the incidents of her childhood. It was a morning in May, in the year 1789,

when she was fifteen years old, and her father was away
in England and she had been left all alone with her step-
mother:

I set off to the woods about a mile from home, and
soon found an outlet to a meadow, and a chestnut tree
attracted my attention, and when I came to it I found rich
moss at the foot. There, then, was a soft seat; the sun
was warm, the air still, and a clear blue vault above; and
all around I heard the numberless sounds of the joy and
melody of spring. The sweet clover and wild flowers I
had gathered by the way were in my hand. I was filled
with love of God and admiration, enthusiastic even, of his
works. I can still recall many sensations that my soul felt
at the moment. I thought my father did not care for me—
well, God was my Father, my all. I prayed, sang hymns,
cried, laughed and talked to myself of how far He could
place me above all sorrow. There I lay still to enjoy the
heavenly peace that came over my soul, and I am sure I
grew, in the two hours so passed, ten years in my spiritual
life. Well all this came vividly to my mind this morning,
when, as I tell you, the body let the spirit alone. I had
prayed and cried heartily (which is my daily and often
hourly comfort), and closing my eyes with my head resting upon my arm on the table, lived all those sweet hours
over again, made myself believe I was again under the
spreading tree. . . .

That was at noon. It was the same night that she
was wakened from her light sleep by the wild sound of the
shipwrecked sailors in the next cell, almost mad with the
cold, who fell into a fight while playing cards and became "as noisy as their anger."

"Patience," writes Elizabeth, in answer to this din. And she adds, by way of having noticed it for the first time, "The Ave Maria bell rings at sunset on one side of us, and on the other tolls the bell 'for the dead' calling to prayer for the souls in purgatory."

And so the life in the Lazaretto went on while the wind roared, the waves boomed, and the cold chilled, while Elizabeth alternated between William's bedside and her Bible, while Anna Maria joined her mother in prayer, or skipped rope, while the imprisoned seamen fought and cursed in the next room and the sentry paced up and down, night and day, carrying his gun.

It is clear that the most perplexed person in the world, because of his experience with these gentle strangers, was the Capitano. ("I am beginning to like my Capitano. He is beginning to understand me.") At first there was no understanding of her. Who was this strange heretic (the most horrible category into which an Italian could put a person) who lived and burned with such faith, such patience, such fortitude in the confines of a dungeon where he had seen strong men take their lives? What was this curious creature imported from beyond the seas, who cried so bitterly every hour, yet ever kept her dignity as an unmistakable lady, who knelt for such long hours in prayer, was so grateful for every least attention or courtesy, and who was always at her Bible (of which she will have read through all the New Testament, and all the Old down to Ezekiel, during her confinement), or singing hymns, and going through the ritual of "her little service," and who, come what may in the way of adversity, would not utter one word of complaint against God?

He had seen such things among the few terribly holy persons of his village in Catholic Italy, and had known of them by hearsay in the cases of the nuns and monks, and from his reading in the lives of the saints. But this woman and her angelic child were not of the Faith. They were Americans, a bad thing to begin with, and heretics, which was worse. And yet he could not deny that there was a quality in their expressions that reminded him of the Madonna at the shrine of his village church, and a valor in their sufferings that he had difficulty in not comparing favorably with his own Catherine of Genoa, or Catherine of Siena. No wonder he often took off his cocked hat, showed his gray hairs, mopped his brow, made a gesture of courtesy and inquired: "Is there anything else I can do for you, Signora?", if only to see the sweet expression of gratitude and independence in her eyes when she replied: "Nothing, my Capitano." You may be sure he had the news of them spread abroad in the town.

Elizabeth, in later life, was to remember her siege in the Lazaretto in terms of one thing chiefly: the death of her husband. I think it would not be unfair, therefore, to review some of the main incidents touching this matter before we close this chapter.

She has already told how thrilling it was for her to know that even at the moments of his greatest distress, she was able to kneel at his side, hold his hand, and raise his soul to make acts of genuine devotion and resignation. "Night and day he calls me his life, his soul, his dearest of women, his all." She seemed to be able actually to pray *in* him.

Half way through the time of their detention, William began to balk, not against her love, but against a regeneration of life and faith to which she urged him with all her strength.

It was true that he had been praying with her, believing with her, calling on the name of Christ with her, during this long agony. But—and this is one of the greatest subtleties by which naturally noble spirits rebel against regeneration or repentance—was it not because he was now faced with death, and was afraid of it, and was using Faith as a subterfuge for what he could not face with his own native courage? Catholic priests know this symptom well, both in the case of converts and of deathbed repentants.

Elizabeth called this resistance a show of "humility." She meant, rather, a show of exaggerated "sincerity," sincerity indeed, but too much of it, bordering (as all the moral virtues do when they are overstressed) on a vice: that of self-sufficiency. "What matter?" a priest would say to a deathbed repentant who might object that the reason he was returning to God was because he was faced with death, and was afraid. "What matter if you are afraid? Is not God meant as much for the afraid as he is for the conceited stoics who think (which is not true) that they can face any adversity with their own strength?" One likes the half impulse not to repent simply because one is dying. But one does not like the "decision" not to do so. Else, where does humility come in, if one is so proud as to maintain that God is to be "chosen" but never "needed"?

"My William's soul," writes Elizabeth, on November 30, the eleventh day of their incarceration, "is so humble, it will hardly embrace the faith which is its resource. At any time we have but our Redeemer, but when the spirit is on the brink, it must cling to Him with increased force, or where is it? Dear William! it is not from an impule of terror you seek your God, you wished to serve Him long before this trial came."

It can be seen from this passage that Elizabeth was using a euphemism when she called her husband's resistance "humble." The word was prompted by her affection for him. The solution she gives accurately: "At any time we have but Our Redeemer, but when the spirit is on the brink, it must cling to Him with increased force."

On December 12, it was almost certain that William would die. "Then came our Capitano, and offered so much kindness." Likewise: "The Doctor had said that . . . if the expectoration from the lungs did not return, he might be gone in a few hours." The Doctor was also distressed to find that Elizabeth, kneeling on a mat, was all alone with her dying husband.

"Well, was I alone?" Elizabeth writes. "Indulgent Father, could I be alone while clinging fast to Thee in continual prayer? . . . I watched all night, sometimes sitting by the fire, sometimes lying down; often I thought the breathing stopped, and kissed his poor face to feel if it was cold."

Dr. Tutilli, upon having examined the patient, said it was not he who was wanted, but that Elizabeth must send for him who would minister to her husband's soul. This was arranged through the kindness of Mr. Filippo Filicchi, who came next morning with Reverend Mr.

Hall, the Protestant clergyman at Leghorn. Shortly before he came, however, the desired discharge from the lungs had occurred. William was breathing much more freely, and was able to follow the prayers said in his behalf.

To wait on Him [God] in my William's soul and body; to console, to soothe those hours of pain and affliction, weariness and watching, which, next to God, I alone can; to touch the cheerful notes of Christian hope and triumph which from his partial love he hears with most pleasure from me, because to me he attributes the greatest share of their consoling influence; to hear him, when he pronounces the name of his Redeemer, declare that I first taught him the sweetness of the sound. Oh! if I were even in the dungeon of this Lazaretto, I would thank God for these days of retirement and seclusion from the world which have afforded opportunity for so blessed a work.

In reading these extracts from Elizabeth's "Journal," and in others I shall quote presently, it is difficult at times to remember that they were written by one who was still a Protestant. Some passages at least must certainly rank with the greatest spiritual writing ever produced in America. Yet I feel I must insert here a brief *caveat*. As the record of a soul's journey out of the darkness toward the light of God's Truth, Elizabeth's writings stand unrivalled in our literature, but we must not expect strict theological accuracy at this stage of her life. Now that she has been canonized, there will be a tendency to regard everything she ever wrote as bearing the stamp of authentic Catholic Truth, but this inclina-

tion will be as mistaken as it will be grossly unfair to
Elizabeth herself.

The "Journal" was first published in 1817, without
Elizabeth's knowledge or permission, when she had been
a Catholic for some years and was already the superior
of a growing religious community. At the time it was
thought that the Rev. Henry Hobart had arranged for it
to be issued, but recent biographers have tended to doubt
this. At any rate its publication caused Elizabeth acute
displeasure and embarassment. She disliked its unortho-
dox opinions and "pious Protestant expressions," as she
put it. If some of the beauty and ardor of the "Journal"
seem tarnished by these comments, I must humbly beg
the reader's pardon, but we would not be doing justice
to Elizabeth's greatness or her sanctity by failing to put
these extracts in their proper perspective.

But even when you have an invisible hand tearing
off the pages from a calendar, he must, unless he be
working in eternity, not in time, come to an end. And so
deliverance from the Lazaretto finally arrived. Dr. Tutilli approved, with the stipulation, however, that William
be moved immediately to the warm air of Pisa, to compensate (ironically) for the damp cold days in the dungeon. And so on Monday morning, December 19, the
bolts were drawn, the gate opened, and amidst a large
and gaping crowd of sightseers a pale American woman,
with her invalided husband and undernourished child,
walked silently out of the confines of the Lazaretto.

Everyone in the town had heard of them, everyone
was anxious to see them; and it being a seasonable hour
(the hour of eleven, just when the Italians begin to feel

the morning is over and the afternoon begun) William, borne on the arms of two men, Elizabeth holding his hand with one hand, and that of her Anna Maria, doll abreast, with the other, made their exit before the curious crowd at the gate. By a combination of ship-voyage and dungeon-detention, they had been exactly seventy-nine days in confinement. They must have presented a pitiful spectacle, so white, so bewildered, so afraid. Mr. Filicchi's coach had been sent to conduct them to Pisa. And as the crowd caught a glimpse of Elizabeth with her gasping husband and her frail daughter, they burst, one and all, into a plaintive cry of sympathy as only the Italians can: "O poverino!"

The old Capitano, tears in eyes, his cocked-hat removed in reverence and respect, and his heart catching a bit in the knowledge that he was unlikely ever to have such exquisite visitors in his dungeon again, mopped his brow, sighed a long sigh, and returned to the management of the captives still in his keeping. And as he issued to the guard and sentries the latest orders of the day, he could hear the voices of peasant folk hailing the carriage of Signor Filicchi as it rolled slowly down the street. "O poverino! O poverino!"

A Dream

*W*illiam Seton was to live exactly eight days after his removal from the Lazaretto. Dr. Tutilli, knowing well that the case was hopeless, had—for we go on clinging to hope even when there isn't any—prescribed that the invalid be brought to Pisa, where there was an especially good climate and cheerful surroundings, with, of course, the River Arno to gaze upon, about which famous river Elizabeth remarks ironically "I had cherished many poetical visions." But to Pisa it must be, and the Brothers Filicchi were quick to secure them favorable lodgings. The distance from Leghorn to Pisa is fifteen miles.

Set up now in the clean, sunny rooms of their boarding establishment at Pisa, the drama of the dark, cold Lazaretto continued to go on. Externally there was a change of surroundings. In their souls there brooded the same travail. Elizabeth was to say at the time of her husband's death that she had not slept for one single moment of the sojourn there, and often would not eat for twenty-four hours at a time. Yet, strangely, William's soul, despite his intense, growing weakness, continued to become more and more courageous, more and more eager not only to die in Christian fashion, but to give himself without complaint to God. There was an agreement between them that if he lapsed into a state where he could not speak, but still retained consciousness, if he still felt love and trust and faith in Christ, he was to press her hand. She had the immense joy of having it happen just that way.

Their reaction to the elegant, comfortable surroundings was at first a merry one. They began to laugh, as one will do, at the miseries they had borne together and their happy deliverance. Wouldn't it be a story to tell to the folks back in America! Wouldn't it be a tale to hand on to their grandchildren! They compared the past and the present and went on to talk "of heavenly hopes," and then prepared to go to sleep—a good one, comfortable, clean, and warm. But no sooner had Elizabeth arranged herself for the night and put pillows and a coverlet on the sofa so she could lie beside him, than the spasms, the vomiting, the suffocation began again. There was no rest that night. This was their first day in Pisa.

On the following day, as petulant invalids will, William insisted on going for a ride in the carriage. A new doctor, Dr. Cartelach, said no, said he might die in the attempt. But William insisted. Elizabeth and the doctor had a conference and it was agreed that "opposition was worse than the risk." So up came the lackeys from the boarding-house, the carriage was ordered, and William was carried down stairs on a chair. The ride lasted five minutes. "O my God!" said Elizabeth, "well did you strengthen me in that hour." "That hour" is priceless.

Of the third day only this is said: it was "cloudy, but quiet."

On the fourth day William must ride again. It could hardly be now a symptom of perverseness, after the five minutes' experience two days before. It was probably a symptom of suffocation. "Claustrophobia" is its name, in our own day, when frightening terms are discovered for very old diseases. The ride this time is most touching, chiefly for Elizabeth's comment on it. William "returned in better spirits and more able to keep himself than when we went out." The landlady went with them. And with that typical humility of an innocent soul, anxious if it can to correct its own judgments in terms of what anyone else has held, Elizabeth adds: "I really begin to think that riding out must be good for him." How nice to find William right and oneself wrong!

But they never rode out again.

On the day before Christmas William was prostrate. Laudanum seemed to be the only medicine the doctor could think of prescribing for the sick man in his spells. William said a strange thing to Elizabeth on this day. He said he thanked God he had been given so much time to reflect before his (he did not mention the word) death. At midnight on Christmas Eve Elizabeth went over to his bed to find him wide awake.

"Are you not asleep, my William?"

"No, love, for the sweetest reflections keep me awake; Christmas Day is begun, the day of our Redeemer's birth."

He turned wearily on his pillow, and why he said the next thing, I cannot for the life of me imagine.

"How I wish we could have the Sacrament!"

Elizabeth's answer is equally enigmatical.

"Well, we must do all we can," she said.

And she put a portion of wine in a glass, and said different parts of the Psalms, and some prayers of her own, and they consumed the cup of Thanksgiving, "setting aside the sorrow of time in view of eternity."

And later, on Christmas morning William insisted that Captain O'Brien of *The Shepherdess* be sent for. Captain O'Brien of *The Shepherdess* was sent for, and came—hat in hand, eyes full of sympathy. With absolute composure, that made Elizabeth shudder, William Seton asked Captain O'Brien if he would do him the great honor and service of conveying his wife and daughter safely back to America. Captain O'Brien bowed his head. He did not ask "in the event of what?" He WOULD, sir! So help him God! That was the big happening of Christmas Day for the Setons that year. There was no Christmas dinner. William took only his drugs, and Elizabeth recorded, "I did not take a mouthful all that day, which was passed on my knees by his bedside."

On the day after Christmas, Elizabeth had another dream. It occurred while her head was resting on the chair by which she knelt, insensibly lost in sleep. And in her slumber she saw "a little angel with a pen in one hand and a sheet of pure white paper in the other. He looked at me, holding up the paper, and wrote in large letters JESUS." She awoke with a start, and whispered it all to William and he "was very much affected when I told him of it."

The night of December 26 was the last William spent on this earth. Elizabeth knelt by his side reading prayers, prayers, prayers. William did not speak through the early part of the night and into the morning, though at times he would stretch out his arms to his Saviour.

"Jesus, Jesus, Jesus," he would say when he began to speak.

(*Then more prayers and prayers and prayers.*)

William: "My Christ Jesus, have mercy!"

(*More prayers and prayers, from Elizabeth on her knees.*)

William: (and at each interruption, Elizabeth stops praying) "Tell all my dear friends not to weep for me. I die happy satisfied with the Divine Will."

(*More prayers and prayers and prayers.*)

William: (remembering his four children over the seas) "Oh, my dear wife, my little ones!"

(*Elizabeth moistens his lips with a handkerchief.*)

William: "My love, did the angel write *Jesus?*"

Elizabeth: "Yes, he did."

Then came a long silence!

"At a quarter past seven on Tuesday morning, December 27th," writes Elizabeth in her journal, "my poor husband gave his last sigh, with the strong pressure of the hand which he had agreed to give me at this moment if his soul continued in its peace with our Jesus."

Little Anna—now called Annina, because the Italians named her so—was brought in, and she and her mother knelt by the bedside and prayed. And were resigned.

The servants were called, but none would come in. Not even the landlady. Not they! How did they know the man did not have the yellow fever? He had just come out of quarantine. And so Elizabeth was left— with the distant assistance of two women who laundered for her—to wash and dress alone the body of her dead husband. She had been doctor and nurse to him. Now she would be undertaker.

In recounting the events leading up to William's death, Archbishop Seton makes a significant comment about his grandfather. William Seton had, says the Archbishop, long felt a secret sympathy for the Catholic religion, as a result of his previous acquaintance with the Filicchi brothers. The Archbishop does not elaborate further, but perhaps we may at least hope that, by God's grace, William's secret yearnings did not go unanswered.

Eventually Mrs. Filicchi's carriage arrived, and Elizabeth was taken off with Annina to Leghorn. Guess who stayed with the corpse that night while it was awaiting burial? Luigi, the poor servant of the Filicchis who had consented to go into quarantine with them while they were confined in the Lazaretto. Tears in his eyes, Luigi.

The next morning at eleven, in the Protestant burying-ground in Leghorn, Elizabeth's "poor clay was laid in the grave." She had one phrase to say as he was being lowered into the earth: "O my Father and my God!"

For consolation, when she turned to him, the Reverend Mr. Hall, who presided at the interment, had this to offer to her: "Whether the tree falls to the south or to the north, and in whatever place it falleth, there shall it lie!"

The Capitano arrived late with black band around his arm and hat, weeping and saying, "Poor Signora!"

And somebody whispered along the way, and Elizabeth overheard it: "If she were not a heretic she would be a saint." In view of the place, the people, and the circumstances, it was about the highest compliment that could be paid.

A Widow

And so this pale widow and her child marched into the magnificent palace of the Filicchis to bide there till the next boat would take them home. How pale she was at this moment can easily be surmised by those of us who have followed her hardships and her anguish since she left the shores of America. And it must also be remembered that on top of the voyage in *The Shepherdess* and the detainment in the dingy Lazaretto, even in the comfortable quarters at Pisa, she had had no sleep and almost no food for the past week. In addition she was—as all sensitive souls are—exceptionally given to tears, for which she had plenty of excuse during the past fortnight. And tears make the body limp and the face dry.

Did she have dresses enough to harmonize with the dazzling establishment into which she was now entering? Undoubtedly not. But undoubtedly, too, she had, or was provided with, the black habiliment of a widow. The Italians—rigidly liturgical in things of the emotions—would be sure to see to that. Indeed, it was the dress of the Italian widow that she was to adopt for her nuns at a later day when she became the foundress of the Sisters of Charity in America. So, presumably, she was used to it in Italy.

But clothes are a small item to consider when one has quality. And the quality of the young Widow Seton was unmistakably evident to the quality of Italy as soon as she appeared in their midst. In fact it was her triumph to impress them by more than her quality. They actually conceded her the encomium of sanctity, a rare conquest for a "heretic" in the milieu of an all Catholic tradition. She had already heard them whispering about her, "If she were not a heretic she would be a saint," and recorded the oft-repeated remark in her journal.

But first we must say a word about the Filicchis and their palace. Had they a palace? You would think so if you saw the engraving of it preserved in the archives of the Sisters of Charity at Emmitsburg. It fronted the water and could be reached directly by land or by boat. It was a spacious three-story building done in brilliant Italian Renaissance style, containing, I should imagine, close on to a hundred rooms. At the left of it was a large quadrangle separating it from an equally brilliant mansion owned by one Mrs. Baragazzi. At the rear of the quadrangle (which contained flower-beds and carefully tended walks) were two chapels, twins in appearance, one presumably for the Filicchis, the other for the Baragazzis. An esplanade passed between the building and the harbor, edged with a high wall, and with a passageway to the dock, and a flight of steps running down to the boats in case the inhabitants chose to make an excursion by sea.

The inferior furnishings of this *maison haute* can be imagined from the proportions and elegance of the outside. In the private chapel Mass was said every day, for the Filicchis were devout Catholics.

The Filicchis were much loved by the people of Leghorn. Every one of their hundreds of servants and retainers, and of the poor who crowded to their doors each

day blessed the fact that riches were in the hands of such
honorable men. You could, of course, have wanted all
their possessions handed over to the State, and commended your interests to the charity of politicians instead
of to the charity of Christian gentlemen. Would the
politicians of Leghorn have called the poor in at the services of Maundy Thursday, in Holy Week, and washed and
kissed their feet in token of the esteem in which Christ's
poor were held? What sort of social program was this
where a benefactor condescended to kiss the feet of his
beneficiaries?

The people of Leghorn preferred it their way. There
is such a thing as property with responsibility, and no one
knew this better than Filippo Filicchi and his brother, Antonio. And no one knew that they knew it better than the
poor of Leghorn, who not only respected but loved them,
and proved that they loved them by a thousand testi-
monials.

Filippo was the elder of the brothers. He had frequently visited America in the interests of his counting-
house, and had married an American girl, a Miss Mary
Cowper of Boston. They were childless. During his
trips to America, he came to be known to nearly every important personage on this side of the Atlantic. He was a
friend of Washington, Hamilton, Jefferson, Madison,
John Adams, Daniel Carroll of Carrollton, and of John
Carroll, the Bishop of Baltimore. Washington's esteem
for and trust in him was so high that he named him the
Consul-General of the United States at Leghorn. An
interesting arrangement: to name an Italian the American
Consul in his own country. But an arrangement indicative

of the profound confidence Washington had in the integrity and objectivity of Filippo Filicchi.

Antonio Filicchi, the younger brother, had married an Italian (the beloved Amabilia of Elizabeth Seton's heart) and they had several children, one of them named, with characteristic unprovincial generosity, Patrizio. Antonio too had visited America in the interests of his business, and was to prove in every way a most charming host, respectful, understanding, and affectionate. In addition to his charm, his bearing, his manners, his fortune, his blood, he had that climax-quality of the perfect Christian gentleman: holiness.

A good Christian husband can be known in his wife as in himself. Together with her (Amabilia) he reverently attended Mass every day. With her he rejoiced and put on a display on the Church's feast days, and fasted and mortified himself in the seasons of penance. It was Amabilia's custom all during Lent never to eat a bite of food until three o'clock in the afternoon. This meant not only mortification, it meant weakness. Fasting wears one down. So do vigils, as the faces of discalced Carmelite nuns would clearly reveal. Our modern common-senseness and frenzy for vitamins and balanced diets poohpoohs all such practices. And like Ernest Hello's *Homme Médiocre,* calls them "exaggerated." Exaggerated they are indeed, and the saints know it. In fact they intend it: to exaggerate the claims of the spirit over the flesh, which program gives the body, eventually, something of the simplicity, whiteness, and lightness of the soul. Paleness and sanctity go closely together.

So the first thing about the rich Filicchis is this: they

fasted, and it hurt, and it made them weak. But as Amabilia said, and Elizabeth noted down, "She says she offers
her weakness and pain of fasting for her sins, uniting this
mortification with Our Saviour's sufferings." This would
be just the sort of thing that would delight Elizabeth,
who had occasion once, upon being troubled by the statement in Holy Scripture, "I turn to you in fasting, weeping
and mourning," to inquire of her spiritual mentor, the
Reverend Mr. Hobart, what was meant by *fasting*. "He
said," remarks Elizabeth, "something about its being an
old custom, and all that."

Anticipating that Elizabeth's stay in Leghorn would
be very short, and expecting that she would go back to
America on Captain O'Brien's *Shepherdess* as soon as it
was ready to sail—possibly in two weeks' time—the
Filicchis undertook to give Elizabeth as much distraction
and diversion as was possible in her brief respite with
them. And so, shortly after she came to live in the
Filicchi mansion, she and Amabilia set out for Florence
to see its treasures, its churches, its art, its wonders.

Before the effect of this trip on her is described, it
must be explained that Elizabeth was not long in the
house of the Filicchis before there began to take place discussions between herself and her hosts on the subject of
religion.

Naturally, in a household as devout as that of the
Filicchis, where prayers were an essential part of the
budget of the day, where every morning was begun with
Holy Mass, where the Rosary was an official part of the
routine, and where, as an out-flowering of all this Faith,
reigned charity, gentleness, and peace, Elizabeth began

to make inquiries. She began to ask about this and that. And what could one do but give answers? The challenge of the Filicchi household was not what they "argued," but what they lived. And Elizabeth was very quick to discover that what they *lived* was, though in externals the same, in essentials quite different from the regimen she had been enticed to by the charm and eloquence of the Reverend Mr. Hobart.

For one thing they believed that in their chapel God resided not in metaphor but in truth. Does this fact, or the absence of it, mean nothing to a soul so intense on appropriating the objective realities of Faith?

"If she were not a heretic she would be a saint." What did this seemingly snooty remark mean on the lips of her admirers in Leghorn? Could they not have said "She *is* a saint" and be done with it? They could not. And it is not difficult to see why.

Sanctification in the fullest Christian meaning of the term is a partnership between the Grace of God and the coöperation of the human will. It is not enough to be good. One must be God-like. And one cannot become God-like by one's own efforts. One must be put surely in touch with the instruments of divinization dispensed to the world through the Incarnation of God Himself. What is Christianity without Jesus and Mary? And Jesus and Mary were precisely the two realities which were being kept from Elizabeth in the sect to which she at present subscribed. It was not her fault, I admit. But, as I happened to say once in a verse:

Not to be able to be blamed for not having a thing
   is not

A very good measure of what we are lacking and
what we have got.

To begin with, Jesus was kept from her most poign-
antly by her complete deprivation of Him in the Blessed
Sacrament. The only "Blessed Sacrament" she knew was
the metaphorical, commemorative reception of Him in
her "little service," effected by the recitation of a few
prayers and the drinking of plain wine, without priest,
without altar, without sacrifice. And as for Mary, there
was a truth whose name was scarcely if ever mentioned in
Elizabeth's religious circle. Nor was ever the full signifi-
cance of the Redemption brought home to her, since it
was Antonio Filicchi who first taught her to make the
Sign of the Cross.

"This evening, standing by the window with the
moon shining full on Mr. Filicchi's countenance, he raised
his eyes to Heaven and showed me how to make the sign
of the Cross. Dearest Rebecca, I was cold with the awful
impression my first making it gave me. The sign of the
cross of Christ on me! Deepest thoughts came with it of
I know not what earnest desires to be closely united with
Him who died on it." (From her Journal of March 18,
1804.)

It was obvious, therefore, that if Christ wanted to
effect a Christianity in her in its fullest and unequivocal
sense, that Grace should arouse her to a knowledge of
Christ and His Blessed Mother as personal realities, not
merely as ideologies. What is Christ to the Christian
Church if He has failed us in the Sacrament of the altar;
and what the Virgin Mary if she has ceased to be the

transcendent Mother of men? That the pattern of Elizabeth's conversion was molded around these two facts is abundantly evident from the happenings at Leghorn and Florence, and from all the notes she was so avidly committing to her Journal day by day. The outcome of the program was to be that the Church which was to secure her these two facts as dogmas, not as polite considerations, was ultimately to be the Church of her choice, the Church of her heart. But of course this was to take some time in the accomplishment. It was even to require, as we shall see, that the ship that was to take her home to America should turn back and debark her again for a longer association with the Filicchis.

For a realization of what the Madonna meant to Christian Europe in its grandest days, there was no better place to go than to Florence. And so, Elizabeth went there for a visit, accompanied by Amabilia. The recital of her stay in Florence amounts to a veritable pageant of the glories of the Virgin Mother: in the Church of the Santissima Annunziata, in the Church of San Lorenzo, where the words of Our Lady's Magnificat came into her mind "with a fervor which absorbed every other feeling," in the Church of Santa Maria, where before a picture of the Descent from the Cross she remarked: "Mary, at the foot, well expressed in her agonized countenance that the iron had entered hers. How hard it was to leave that picture."

Annina, who had gone with them to Florence, punctuated the visit with one of her notable remarks. She had been and would continue to be a constant source of consolation and joy to her mother throughout their sojourn in Italy. On a visit to the royal gardens, Annina said, upon seeing the Queen (Maria-Louisa of Spain, widow of Louis of Parma) that "she would not be known from any other woman but by the number of her attendants." Whether or not Annina acquired a distaste for temporal queens after seeing with her mother so many brilliant pictures of the Queen of Heaven (whose attendants were invariably angels) I do not know. But at any rate if the Setons were unaware of the extent to which Christian devotion can go in honoring and depicting the Mother of God, the error was remedied during their sojourn in Florence, where from hundreds of shrines and from hundreds of portraits, in all attitudes and in every phase of the mysteries with which she was overwhelmed, Our Lady stood staring at them, and not least of all in the brilliant galleries of the Uffizi and the Pitti Palace, where some of her most lovely images in paint and in stone are dispensed.

It was while she was in Florence in the company of his wife, Amabilia, that Elizabeth received the following message from Antonio Filicchi.

Pardon me, my virtuous friend, if I trouble you with these few lines. Your dear William was the early friend of my youth; you are now come in his room. May the good Almighty God enlighten your mind and strengthen your heart to see and follow, in religion, the surest, true way to eternal blessings. I shall pray for you; I must meet you in Paradise if it is decreed that the vast plains of ocean shall soon be between us. Do not discontinue meanwhile to pray, to knock at the door.

Your most affectionate and respectful friend and servant,

Anthony Filicchi.

It was not decreed that the vast plains of ocean should soon be between them, and by a very providential arrangement.

Elizabeth and Anna early in February, 1804, were put safely on board *The Shepherdess* again, entrusted to the protecting care of Captain O'Brien and his wife, bade a fond farewell by the Filicchis, "loaded with their blessings and presents, with gold and passports and recommendations for fear of Algerines or necessity of putting into any Mediterranean port," but all in vain. The vessel after a few hours of voyage struck a driving storm. It crashed into another boat in trying to maneuver its way into the Mediterranean. Captain O'Brien, in all prudence, had to turn back to the port of Leghorn. To make matters worse, the child Anna took desperately sick, running a high fever. To make matters still worse, O'Brien could not get a bill of health allowing them to depart. There was no sense in their crossing the ocean in this condition. So back they went, welcomed with the sincerest charity, by the Filicchis, yet mightily disappointed; for remember, there were four little Setons waiting anxiously on the other side of the Atlantic, who had not seen their Anna since she became an orphan, nor their mother since she became a widow. In addition, Rebecca Seton, Elizabeth's half soul, to whom all the notes in Elizabeth's journal were directed, was seriously ill, indeed, was to survive for only a short time after the return to America.

But one does what one can, and one could not sail back
to one's native shores under the circumstances which
had arisen. Upon consulting a physician about Anna's
illness, Elizabeth was told she must either give up the
voyage or the life of the child.

So back to the Filicchi mansion again, to be showered
with tenderness and attention, to be sure, but to feel the
keen disappointment of not hurrying to one's dear ones at
the time when they most needed her. And, as though all
crosses must come her way in the process of her purification and sanctification, Elizabeth fell ill herself of the
fever Anna had contracted, and suffered the crisis that
occurs in such things, during which her life was almost,
though not quite, despaired of. The Filicchis doubled
their prayers and Amabilia her penances. Everything that
could be done for them in the way of doctors, nurses,
medicines, was done. And eventually both mother and
child were eased into a happy convalescence and fitted to
make their second attempt to cross the Atlantic when the
time would come for it.

Antonio Filicchi, eager to bring Elizabeth's precious
soul into the fold of the Faith, without which safeguard
it would surely have floundered in the face of all it must
yet endure, had a long brief of the credentials and doctrines of the Catholic Church drawn up for her by the
hand of a young priest of Gubbio, a Father Joseph Pecci
(son of Count Pecci) and member, I believe, of the famous family from which Leo XIII was to come. It is an
accurate syllabus of all Catholic teaching. Antonio trans-
lated it into English for Elizabeth's greater ease in studying it; and there is no doubt that it impressed her, though

she gave no indications at this time of becoming a Catholic.

No indications except her intense preoccupation with those two beautiful mysteries so dear to the hearts of her new Catholic friends: the Blessed Virgin, and the Blessed Sacrament.

One day she found a prayer-book of Mrs. Filicchi's on the table. Unbidden she opened it, and the first thing her eye fell upon was Saint Bernard's prayer to the Blessed Virgin, begging her to be Our Mother. Elizabeth began reciting the prayer to herself, and adds:

I said it to her with such a certainty that God would assuredly refuse nothing to His Mother, and that she could not help loving and pitying the poor souls he died for, that I truly felt I had a Mother, which you know my foolish heart so often lamented to have lost in early days. From the first remembrance of infancy I have looked, in all the plays of childhood and wildness of youth, to the clouds for my mother, and at that moment it seemed as if I had found more than her, so I cried myself to sleep on her heart.

It is not known whether Reverend Mr. Hobart would call this beautiful apostrophe an unnecessary part of "the sumptuous worship of Italy," but at any rate, in making it Elizabeth took a strong step away from the bleak, Madonna-less Trinity Church, and a strong one back to the Faith of her fathers.

But even more significant than this sudden attachment to Our Lady—or rather, one should say significant because of it—was Elizabeth's profound attraction for the Mystery of the Blessed Sacrament, that most exquisite Body formed by the Love of the Holy Ghost in the womb of a little Jewish Virgin, delivered into its state of natural life in the crib of Bethlehem, and into its state of Eucharistic life on the table of the Last Supper.

The first challenge of this Sacred Mystery came to her in a most startling and dramatic way. She was attending Mass in the Benedictine Monastery of Monte-Nero, called the Sanctuary of the Madonna, and situated on a pretty hill just outside Leghorn. Annina was with her, and both the Filicchi families. Her eyes had become enraptured by the painting of Our Lady which is kept there, a work of Greek origin, in which Our Blessed Mother is seated on a richly ornamented cushion, with the Infant Jesus on her left, who holds in one hand a string, at the end of which is attached a little bird that rests on the right arm of His Mother.

But they had come not so much to see the Virgin's picture as to hear Mass. Besides, the monastery was especially sacred to Filippo Filicchi. The kindly monks had once kept him in hiding there when his life was threatened in one of the political uprisings in Italy.

Mass had begun, and the priest had come to the moment of Consecration. The chapel was hushed, and all the worshipers had bowed their heads. The priest spoke the words of the Consecration and was lifting the Sacred Host aloft for the people to adore, when a young Englishman, a sightseer, kneeling directly behind Elizabeth, leaned over and whispered in her ear: "This is what they call their Real Presence!"

This remark, Elizabeth declared, "brought the blood

from my very heart to my face." . . . And she adds:
"My very heart trembled with shame and sorrow for his
unfeeling interruption of their sacred adoration, for all
around was dead silence, and many were prostrated. In-
voluntarily I bent from him to the pavement, and thought,
with starting tears, of the words of St. Paul: 'They discern not the Lord's Body'; and the next idea that came
quickly into my head was, how they could eat and drink
their own damnation for not discerning it, if indeed it is
not there. Yet how could it be there, and how did He
breathe my soul into me, and how—and how—a hundred
other things I know nothing about?"

There is, as we see, no real act of Faith yet. But
Grace will be persistent and the Hound of Heaven will
pursue. For only a week later we find her on the same
subject again in her Journal.

"My sister," she exclaims again to Rebecca, "how
happy we would be if we believed what these good souls
believe, that they *possess* God in the Sacrament, and that
He remains in their churches, and is carried to them when
they are sick. Ah me! When they carry the Blessed
Sacrament under my window, while I feel the full loneliness and sadness of my case, I can not stop the tears at
the thought."

The Flamingo

There now occurs in the career of Elizabeth Seton a crisis in which the daring quality of Christian love is put to a strong test.

The Shepherdess, with its benevolent and courteous Captain O'Brien and his solicitous wife had—as we already know—sailed for America without Elizabeth and her child. There was no thought on this voyage, were it to have been consummated, of her needing any companionship, any protection. There was something too clear in the eyes of Captain O'Brien to indicate that precautions of this kind, where he was concerned, were necessary. *The Shepherdess,* with Elizabeth and Anna Seton on board, had already departed, had been buffeted and defeated in its first few hours of voyage, and had perforce deposited both mother and child back again on the dock of Leghorn, and had found them unfitted by the quarantine regulations for departure. They were most welcome once more in the household of the Filicchis, as we have seen. Annina was ill, and Elizabeth was on the point of becoming so. "You would say," commented Elizabeth concerning the Filicchis' generosity, "that it was Our Lord himself they received, in his poor sick strangers."

But the second departure (on April 8, 1804) was to be on another boat called *The Flamingo.* The Setons, Elizabeth and Anna Maria, were to be the only passengers. The Captain was not a Catholic, possibly not even a Christian. His name was Blagg (a dangerous name, if

you follow symbolism in the matter of nomenclature).
Who was this Captain Blagg? Was he respectable? Was
he courteous, reliable? Was he a gentleman? In certain
emergencies, possibly so. But was he such in the case of an
attractive young widow with whom he was to live alone
on the high seas for an indefinite number of days? Elizabeth had only mild apprehensions, remarking that this
Captain was "a very young man and a stranger." But the
Filicchis had more profound doubts. And it was Amabilia
(the well named wife of Antonio) who settled them. Antonio, so Amabilia decided, should accompany this mother
and child to America on the small ship that Captain Blagg
commanded.

Amabilia must have been terribly sure of her Antonio, to say that she would entreat him to fulfil such a
commission. But so she did. And in such a gorgeous,
trustful, and Christian manner.

Now here is a problem. Was Antonio Filicchi in
love with Elizabeth Seton? It is unquestionably true that
he was. But it was a love of reverence and admiration, not
one of possession. It could be daringly achieved in chastity and courtesy, because he knew the meaning of his
marriage vow. And nobody appreciated this more than
his "loved one," his Amabilia. And it was she who sent
him to cross to America on *The Flamingo* in the company
of a woman who in any less delicate association would
have been her rival. What Antonio was to do and fulfil
in the course of this voyage, and the exquisiteness of his
gallantry, his honor, his purity, his fidelity, are shown by
the fact that from then till the hour of her death—yes,
even when she was to be a most disciplined and asceticized

nun, he was to remain to her until the very last breath of her life her "dearest brother, her dearest Antonio." Let the prudish, Jansenized Christian (Catholic or otherwise) take this problem and solve it as he may. At any rate, in Amabilia's heart it was a choice between the assumed moral rectitude of one Captain Blagg, and the assured honor and integrity of her husband, Antonio. She made the second choice. In it she distinguished herself both as a lover and a wife.

"My sister," Antonio said to her, "Almighty God takes care of little birds, and makes the lilies of the field to grow, and you feel He will not take care of you? I tell you He *will* take care of you." And He did. And Antonio Filicchi, Italian nobleman, was not the least instrument in effecting this Providence on God's part.

On the morning of their departure the cannon of *The Flamingo* boomed two hours before sailing time, to let her passengers know that they must soon assemble. The Filicchis celebrated the event by attendance at Mass. Elizabeth tells us in her diary: "Mrs. Filicchi came while the stars were yet shining brightly, to say that we would go to mass, and she would then part with her Antonio. Oh! the admirable woman! . . . My Saviour! my God! Antonio and his wife—their communion, poor I, not; but I did beg Him to give me their faith, and promised Him *all* in return for such a gift. . . . Antonio and Amabilia, their separation in God; her last adieu on the balcony, where we stood as the sun rose full upon us, and the final signal from the vessel hurried us apart, will I ever forget?"

And so out of the harbor of Leghorn, under the protection of a friend's husband, sailed Anna and Elizabeth, on board *The Flamingo* with its dangerous Captain Blagg. And no harm came to them. The voyage was routine. There were long talks during the trip, and discussions about the Christian Faith, and about the realities of Jesus and Mary.

The child Anna's remark as they were about to sail, was again thoroughly characteristic. "Ma," she said, "are there no Catholics in America? Ma, won't we go to the Catholic church when we go home?" These were provoking questions. Elizabeth tried not to listen to them. But perforce she had to. The simplicity of her young daughter was putting in her mind the very questions she knew she ought to ask herself—if she dared.

Early in June, after nearly a two months' voyage, Captain Blagg pulled down his sails, and deposited Elizabeth, Anna, and Antonio safely in New York. The latter had immediately to go to Boston on business, but the influence of his counsel and his example had been deeply stamped on Elizabeth's mind during the days of the journey. He knew, and she knew, that there was still something tremendously weak in her, something that Grace had not yet conquered. It symbolized itself entirely around the personality of Reverend Mr. Hobart. She was not only in awe of him, she was positively afraid of him. To her dying sister-in-law, Rebecca, she could confide without fear the attraction which the Catholic Faith had for her. But Hobart was the stumbling block which was to delay her conversion until all points of "honor" and "loyalty" (points on which he was to harp with a loud clangor) were settled.

Not long before her arrival in New York we find her anticipating him in her diary. She knew the ordeal to come when she was to face him, his somber clothes, his charm, and his Evangelical eloquence, with the suggestion that she should want to embrace the Faith of Rome.

Here is what she says: "As I approach to you I tremble, and while the dashing of the waves and their incessant motion picture to me the allotment which God has given me, the tears fall fast through my fingers at the insupportable thought of being separated from you. . . . You will not be severe, you will respect my sincerity, and although you will think me in error, and even reprehensible in changing my religion, I know that heavenly Christian charity will plead for me in your affections. . . . Still, if you will not be my brother, if your dear friendship and esteem must be the price of my fidelity to what I believe to be the truth, I can not doubt the mercy of God who will certainly draw me nearer to Himself; and this I confidently feel from experience of the past and the truth of His Promises which can never fail."

It is all right to speak such words to one's diary. But to face in person an engaging Protestant Minister, who has specialized on one as the chiefest worshiper in his congregation, and who has the most engaging method of making "loyalty" much more attractive than "faith," is quite another thing. Antonio Filicchi knew as much when he chivalrously deposited Elizabeth and her child on the dock at Manhattan, went to attend to his business affairs, and prayed in union with his Amabilia that the promise of conversion already recognized in Elizabeth, might be, even despite the suave arguments of Mr. Hobart (who would take her change of faith as a personal insult), realized for the Glory of God and the great need of the Catholic Church in the United States of America.

An Ordeal

Elizabeth and her child arrived safely in New York. Filicchi left them, to attend to business in Boston. She rushed to embrace her four children, who had been distributed among relatives and friends. And in the shelter of various hospitalities she began to figure out how she must henceforth exist, seeing that she knew what her husband did not know (and was not let know) before his death, that their business interests had collapsed and that they were all but paupers. William had made an exorbitant will disposing of a this and a that which the Italian doctors thought it best not to let him know he did not possess.

This was the very worst time in the world to be thinking about a conversion to the Catholic Faith, an act which would fly in the face of practically all those to whom Elizabeth might turn in her difficulties for sympathy and support. Prudentially the thought of such a thing at the moment was ridiculous. It was impractical, rash, absurd; which is sometimes the indication of a thing's being from a supernatural, not a natural, source. For Grace, particularly the Grace of conversion, which is the result not of argument, not of reading, not of personal persuasion, not of conscience, of sense of obligation, not even of apologetic evidence (though these enterprises "prepare" the way), is often impractical, rash, and absurd, judged by any temporal standards. This Grace of Faith does not take into account one's economic situation, one's health, one's domestic troubles, one's temporal loyalties, not even one's life or death. The "He that hateth not father and mother, yea, and his own life also cannot be my disciple," was spoken by Our Lord, not to indicate a coldness of heart toward one's loved ones in the achievement of Faith, but that its impact is made independently of any human or mundane consideration. The result of a conversion is as likely to be starvation or martyrdom as it is to be temporal security or practical comfort.

Some readers may protest—and by every natural standard they have a right to do so—that it is special pleading to claim that Elizabeth's conversion to the Catholic Faith, and not her excellence of goodness and character, was the all-important factor in her life. Yet that claim is but following the evidence in the case. When she was a tired, middle-aged nun, wasting away with weariness and disease, and was asked what was the greatest favor God had ever bestowed on her, she was to reply: "My grace of conversion to the Catholic Faith." And shall we outlaw her own statement of her career (and who was to understand herself better than herself?) simply because it fits in with what we want and believe to be true?

There is, however, a relationship between the supernatural and the natural in the matter of Grace that needs to be explained. It is absolutely true that Grace fulfills and does not destroy nature, just as the New Testament fulfilled the Old. The Catholic Faith began, inchoatively, in the Garden of Eden, when God promised sinful man a Redeemer to come who would, by His sufferings and merits, excuse the world of its wickedness. That Redeemer *has* come and, as someone has aptly said of those who still attend His coming, "They are like men sitting in an abandoned railway station waiting for a train which passed years ago."

But this much is also true. Despite the fact that Grace enhances every human love and affection, and that a convert to Catholicism loves the things and persons he has left more intensely than before (for all that he seems to reject them), where supernature does not in the least abound, but only personal integrity and "character," because, as Tertullian said, "Anima humana est naturaliter Christiana," there is an inborn tendency in each one of us to "compensate" through natural goodness for what Faith has not yet supplied, and to strain toward a Grace-life which has not yet arrived. And this is particularly shown, in the case of heretics, by the way they overstress (I use the word advisedly) a few of the natural virtues, which give resistance to the Divine, not because these handful of virtues possessed by the heretic are bad *in se* (they are, rather, good), but because they are inadequate, and they presume to compensate for their own inadequacy by attempting to become something that they never can become without the special assistance of God.

So one will find in the ranks of the heretics such things as truth-telling, paying one's debts, fidelity to one's relatives overstressed. It is not in these things that the aim is not good; but the arrow is shot short of the mark. It is infinitely better to tell the truth for Christ's sake than for the sake of one's reputation, one's family heritage, or one's feeling of self-righteousness in the matter.

Likewise, there is a tendency in all the heresies (which strive to impress by moral rather than Grace-righteousness) to unbalance a virtue and make it do service for something it can never do service for. Loyalty is one thing. Faith is entirely another. The one is a behavior in a human way toward one's equals. The other is a behavior in a super-human way (and through the mind—the greatest of man's faculties) toward the everlasting, immutable, and all adorable God.

It is not surprising, therefore, to find Reverend Mr. Hobart (to whom Elizabeth in "loyalty" had recourse immediately upon her return to New York) harping on every motive which would appeal to her as being "honorable," "loyal," "true to your tradition," etc. He will never once discuss the objective evidence of Catholic Christianity whether Scriptural or otherwise—dismissing the whole matter of the Faith which the Confessors preached, the Virgins honored, and for which the Martyrs died with the phrase: it is "a communion which my sober judgment tells me is a corrupt and sinful communion." On what score, he does not say.

His leading card is that she should not abandon "the simple but affecting worship of Trinity Church," as though sumptuousness and elegance in the matter of adoration were an evil. "This might have been sold and given to the poor" is a compelling phrase until one remembers who first spoke it: Judas Iscariot, who sold Christ for thirty pieces of silver.

Mr. Hobart's apologetic against the proposed aberration of his most gifted penitent takes the following course:

"You may naturally conclude that the subject on which I now address you is deeply interesting to me. . . ."

"I can not be otherwise than deeply affected. . . ."

"When I see one, too, from whose friendship myself and many others have derived, and have hopes always to continue to derive, comfort, and pleasure, in danger of taking a step which in its consequences may separate her from our society which in times past was her solace and enjoyment, it would be strange indeed if my anxious sensibilities were not awakened. . . ."

"If it should appear that you have forsaken the religion of your forefathers. . . ."

"You wish, you say, to be informed whether the church in which you have been educated is the church which your Redeemer and His Apostles instituted? Without going into explanations and discussions. . . ."

"There is no necessity for your troubling yourself with the pretensions of other churches. They may be right or they may be wrong. You have been educated in a particular church. You have derived comfort and enjoyment in this church. It is the church in which your forefathers and nearest relatives have gone to rest. . . ."

By such theological side-slants did the Reverend Mr. Hobart seek to avoid the two importunate questions which Elizabeth was always putting to him in relation to the religion she held at the moment. "Is Jesus Christ truly and substantially present in the Blessed Sacrament of the Altar?" "Is Mary truly the Mother of God?"

In the end, Reverend Mr. Hobart did a very wrong thing, even from the point of attack in which he was endeavoring to deter his penitent from taking the step uppermost in her mind. He lost his temper!

Elizabeth's home-coming in regard to her relatives and children is well summarized in her exclamation: "The home of plenty and comfort, the society of sisters united by prayers and divine affections, the evening hymns, the daily readings, the sunset contemplations, the service of holydays together, the kiss of peace, the widow's visits, all, all gone forever. And is poverty and sorrow the only exchange? My husband, my sisters, my house: poverty and sorrow!"

It was a situation, obviously, in which a conversion to the Catholic Faith—the most unconscionable procedure that could happen in the New York milieu of the moment —was unutterably rash, impractical, crazy.

On Sunday morning, July 8, 1804, Rebecca Seton, the beloved sister-in-law of Elizabeth's life, her half-soul, and the confidante of all the diary entries which were written from the time of her departure to Italy until her return, passed away (or, a Catholic would say, "died"). This dear "Protestant Sister of Charity," as she was admiringly called by those anxious to find a designation worthy of her, was undoubtedly as near and dear to Elizabeth's soul in a spiritual way as any creature she was ever to know and love. "Dear, dear soul," Elizabeth exclaims of her, "we shall never more watch on our knees together the setting sun, and sigh for the Sun of righteousness!" And, speaking of her death, at which Elizabeth was present, she says, "I raised her head, and drew her

lightly towards me, Nature gave its last sigh, and she was
gone in five minutes without a groan."

Elizabeth, well used to deathbeds by now, was again
the ultimate comforter, short of God, in this, the death
of her dearest Rebecca. After Rebecca's passing, Elizabeth's correspondence, her diaries, her journals, her remembrances, will be as avid and honest as ever, and her
letters to her son William will be supreme in the expression of mother love. Yet it is undeniable that something
of the spontaneity with which she used to write when Rebecca was to read is henceforth lost. Elizabeth will continue to confide through pen and ink to paper many of
the soul travails of her life till her very last days. Else
we should have no biographies of her as complete as they
are. But it is most evident that the spark, the impulse,
the verve of her writings up to this moment will be altered
from now on. Rebecca is dead. And Rebecca was the only
one to whom one should and could tell *all.*

Did Rebecca's death retard Elizabeth's conversion
to the Catholic Faith? Undoubtedly it did. We can
only bow before the inscrutable designs of God's providence, when He chooses to call from this life so close a
companion and confidante, so much a part of one's own
soul, as it were, as Rebecca was to Elizabeth. Such a
loss cannot but be a profound shock—to anyone, and
especially to one so sensitive as Elizabeth Seton. Was she
really on the path to Divine Truth when God had treated
her so cruelly?

In such ways as this does Our Lord share His Cross
with His chosen ones. Yet life must go on, and there
were important decisions to be made. To begin with,

Elizabeth had five children dependent on her. And to them, if she was not to inoculate them with Christian despair—which is more poignant even than the Oriental form of the same—she must make up her mind whether or not she should teach them that Christ is truly present in the Blessed Sacrament, or is not. This is not "an incidental item" of Christianity; it is practically its heart and soul, its ultimate and intolerant challenge.

"Your Antonio would not have been well pleased to see me in St. Paul's [Protestant Episcopal] Church today," she writes to Amabilia Filicchi in September, 1806, "but peace and persuasion about proprieties, &c. over prevailed: yet I got in a side pew, which turned my face toward the Catholic Church [Old Saint Peter's, Barclay Street] in the next street, and found myself twenty times speaking to the Blessed Sacrament *there,* instead of looking at the naked altar where I was, or minding the routine of prayers."

Also, in regard to such a prayer as the *Hail Mary!* of which Annina Maria was saying to her mother at the moment "Oh do, ma, teach it to us," what was Mr. Hobart to say, if the impropriety were broached to him? Mr. Hobart later became a Bishop. And it is fair to relate that Wilberforce in his *Hist. of Prot. Episc. Church in America,* Chapter IX, was to say: "He had all the mental and moral qualities which make men leaders of their fellows. Undaunted, ready, sagacious, he never abandoned a principle, deserted a friend, or quailed before an enemy." But what was Mr. Hobart to say to Elizabeth if she proposed the practice of teaching her child the Hail Mary? And why was Elizabeth the peculiar *pièce de ré-*

sistance to him at this precise time? Was she an embodiment in an attractive, feminine, un-get-at-able form of the problem with which his own conscience was troubling him? Maybe Mr. George Edmond Ironside, a convert to Catholicism, formerly an Episcopalian, can answer this question.

Writing to Hobart in the year 1820, when Hobart was then a Bishop, and anent the charges of Bishop Hobart's, entitled *Corruptions of the Church of Rome, Contrasted with Certain Protestant Errors,* Ironside remarks, "But now, when you, who have more than once expressed your wish to pass the end of your days in the bosom of the *Roman Catholic Church,* come forth armed with all the dignity and influence of office, it is necessary that you should meet with an answer." There is probably nothing in the world more annoying to a man than to see his own conscience troubling him in the person of a woman whom he respects and admires.

Hobart, not Bishop, but only Reverend Mr. for the moment, began by giving Elizabeth tracts and books against the Church. These she read dutifully. Filippo Filicchi retaliated by giving her other books *for* the Church. He also gave her letters of introduction to Bishops Carroll of Baltimore and Cheverus of Boston. It was a terrible tug-of-war, and it ended up by leaving her neither Catholic nor Protestant.

Her health was none too good. At the end of the summer three of her children were to be taken with the whooping-cough. A most pitiful picture of her religious state at the time is drawn by herself in a letter to Amabilia Filicchi.

"The children are all asleep. This is my time of many thoughts. I had a most affectionate note from Mr. Hobart today, asking me how I could ever think of leaving the church in which I was baptized. But though whatever he says to me has the weight of my partiality for him, as well as the respect it seems to me I could scarcely have for anyone else; yet that question made me smile, for it is like saying wherever a child is born, and wherever its parents place it, it will find the truth. And he does not hear the droll invitations made me every day since I am in my little new home, and old friends come to see me; for it has already happened that one of the most excellent women I ever knew, who is of the Church of Scotland, finding me unsettled about the great object of the true faith, said to me: 'Oh, do, dear soul, come and hear our J. Mason, and I am sure you will join us.' A little after came one whom I loved for the purest and most innocent manners, and belonging to the Society of Friends (to which I have always been attached); she too, coaxed me with artless persuasion: 'Betsy, I tell thee, thee had best come with us.' Then my faithful old friend, Mrs. T. of the Anabaptist meeting says, with tears in her eyes: 'Oh! could you enjoy with us our heavenly banquet': and my good servant Mary, the Methodist, groans and 'contemplates,' as she expresses it, 'my soul so misled because I have yet no convictions.' "

And so it went. Every Sunday morning she was carefully watched to see what church she would attend, or if she would go at all. Someone gave her Newton's *Prophecies* to read, in which she found that all followers of the Pope were consigned to Hell. In an effort to keep peace

among her persuaders and to observe proprieties, she felt
impelled to go to some church or other for worship. "I
got into a side pew which turned my face towards the
Catholic church in the next street, and twenty times found
myself speaking to the Blessed Sacrament *there* . . ."
She was honest with Mr. Hobart about her behavior on
this occasion.

He: "How can you believe that there are as many
gods as there are millions of altars and tens of millions
of sacred hosts all over the world?"

She: "Is it God who does it?"

And so it went on through the autumn months into
the winter. She became thinner and thinner, in fact—and
she was not given to over-description—described herself
as a skeleton. She finally came to believe in nothing, deciding that if she could not find which religion was true,
she would fight through life without any.

The gossip of her friends and relatives continued.
She was the almost exclusive topic of conversation in her
circle whenever the question of religion was brought up.
One might well say—and no one is to be blamed for saying so who views the story of this life as a natural phe-
nomenon, who has never pondered the words of Our
Lord "I came not to bring peace, but the sword"—that
this business of conversion was the most annoying, unwar-
ranted, perplexing affair that had ever entered her life.

In addition to this, she received in October (1804)
a stiff letter of rebuke from her otherwise gentlest of
friends, Antonio.

"I am become very uneasy," he writes, "both for you
and for myself, and I lament very much your imprudence

and mine. Yours, for having resisted the light that had shown you the precipice that you have before your feet; mine, for having exposed you to it by moderating your first zeal. When you left me, no doubts remained in your mind. How imprudent was it then to submit your determination to the censure of people who could not be expected to do otherwise than oppose it, and introduce trouble and disquiet in your conscience to deter you from it!"

But in the meantime there seems to have been no one really who understood Elizabeth's agony and travail but her children. And seeing her, as they often did, lying on her bed, her head bursting with pain, her eyes distorted with doubt, with a volume of Newton on one side and a volume of Saint Francis de Sales on the other, no wonder they often tip-toed in and exclaimed, over and over again, "Poor Mama!"

Old Saint Peter's

Mr. Hobart had spoken of "the sumptuous worship of the Church in Italy." No one could speak at this time of "the sumptuous worship" of Saint Peter's Church in Barclay Street, New York, presided over by two priests, Father Matthew O'Brien, secular, and Father William O'Brien, O.P. (a name, however, which Elizabeth was not likely to resent in view of her *Shepherdess* experience), and attended only by a handful of poor immigrants. The worship in this poor church, aside from the majesty of the Holy Sacrifice of the Mass, might be said to be, in external details, even less pretentious than that held in the church where Henry Hobart reigned by reason of the magnificence of his eloquence and the sterling quality of his character. It is true that in Philadelphia and Baltimore, at this era, there were Catholic services held with much greater décor (not enough to compete with the Italian grandeur, but with enough to resemble it); but New York's Saint Peter's was quite ordinary as far as splendor of material detail and distinction of clientele were concerned. So much so that Elizabeth's advisers against the absurdity of her going over to "such a church" were quick to capitalize on it by way of argument.

The Catholics of New York were called by her well-intentioned discouragers "the offscouring of the people," "a public nuisance," and such like opprobrious designations. "That troubles me not," says Elizabeth, with her characteristic generosity; "the congregation may be very shabby, yet very pleasing to God; or there may be very bad people among it, yet that can not hurt the *faith,* as I take it, and should the priest himself deserve no more respect than is here allowed him, his ministry of the sacraments would be the same to me if . . . I shall ever receive them. I seek but God and His Church, and expect to find my peace in *them,* not in the people."

This is all splendid, and startingly un-Protestant; but still it is many weeks (from January to March, 1805) away from an avowal of the Catholic Faith by way of deliberate profession. The Filicchis, anxious to have their Faith represented to her under the most favorable auspices, were all for having her received into the Church by the brilliant Bishop Cheverus of Boston, or the renowned Bishop Carroll of Baltimore. But it was impractical to leave New York at the time, and even if one went away to be *converted,* one would have to return to *worship.*

In the same month (January, 1805) she could say of herself and her children, "You would not say we are unhappy, for the mutual love with which all is seasoned, can only be enjoyed by those who have experienced our reverse, but we never give it a sigh." How much effort of character there was entailed in "not giving it a sigh" only those of us know who have had to deal with our own introversions and selfishnesses.

"I play the piano in the evening for my children," says Elizabeth, still in the month of January, "and after they have danced themselves tired, we gather round the fire, and I go over with them the scenes of David, Daniel, Judith, or other great characters of the Bible, until we entirely forget the present." Though she was all motherly sweetness to her children, in reality Elizabeth was at this moment going through the greatest spiritual crisis of her life, and she had no one to whom she could turn for aid. It seemed to be God's Will that she work out her decision absolutely alone. Antonio was away in Boston, embroiled in his firm's business, and for some unexplained reason Elizabeth was unable to contact any of the four Catholic priests then in New York.

As the winter wore on, however, her determination grew ever stronger, and as one spiritual obstacle after another fell away, a great peace began to come into her soul. Mr. Hobart's controversial books were laid aside. The strictures of her friends in relation to the low-estate (the house-maid quality) of Catholic worship were adequately dealt with in her mind. The fact that, in becoming a Catholic, she was to lose caste, station, wealth, support, companionship, even æsthetic discernment and good taste, were all rebutted in her mind in terms of the tremendous realities of Catholic Dogma which she was so eagerly seeking. She must have the Blessed Sacrament and Our Lady as realities, or else relinquish all thought of them. There was left only one great stumbling block. Her well-wishers, her spyers, her gossips-against-her, even her spiritual counsellor, were quick to push the point. If she were to become a Catholic, it would mean not only the launching of her own career under such dangerous auspices, but she would also have to take the responsibility for the consciences of her five children who, seeing they admired and adored her so much, would be sure to follow (in their innocence) wheresoever she led. Dare she in a change of religion be accountable to God not only for her own, but for five other immortal souls, orphaned of a father who had died respectably—even courageously— within the fold of the anti-Catholic faith?

Elizabeth was much more aware of this problem than any of her accusers could goad her to be. "Now my friends tell me to take care," she writes, "that I am a mother, and must answer for my children at the judg-ment-seat, whatever faith I lead them to. That being so, I will go peaceably and firmly to the Catholic Church. For if faith is so important to our salvation, I will seek it where true faith first began, will seek it among those who received it from God Himself. The controversies on it I am quite incapable of deciding, and as the strictest Protestant allows salvation to a good Catholic, to the Catholics will I go, and try to be a good one. May God accept my good intention and pity me." And she adds, by way of codicil to this decision, "for if the chief church became Antichrist's, and the second holds her rights from it, then I should be afraid both might be antichristian, and I be lost by following either."

But still the weeks went on. Every morning dawned with a decision in her mind to do something about this "urge," this "call," that was to drive her into association with the "low-brow" worship of Saint Peter's in Barclay Street. Every night ended with an incompletion of this proposed decision. She was young. She had tact, beauty, charm. Many a one of the marriage-minded beaux of New York would have succumbed to her romantic inter-est at this period, had she cared to give it. She was not yet thirty-one, a widow and a mother. The great, good judgment of Saint Thomas More, when he was a young widower seeking his second bride, will testify to the attraction of a woman with these qualities. Elizabeth had every engaging art that could be imagined. She was vivacious, understanding, could be coquettish (if she cared to), had borne five children (not an inconsiderable achievement in the eyes of a prospective husband were he anxious to have bantlings of his own), could dance, play the piano, ride skilfully on horseback. She had added to her other accomplishments that of spiritual charm. It might easily have dawned on her, in view of her poverty, her impending ostracization by everyone to whom she could turn for support, that she might well capitalize her talents in the matter of romance and love, if not for her own sake, for that of her children.

But it did not turn out so. Rather, on the Day of Ash Wednesday, February 27, 1805, she marched resolutely to the Church of Saint Peter in New York (a church which, she remarked, has "a cross on the top instead of a weathercock"), while exclaiming in her heart, "Here, my God I go!"

It was, as has been said, the Day of Ash Wednesday, the beginning of Lent, and as she entered the church, the priest was giving a sermon in which he "talked of death so familiarly that he delighted and revived me."

The ceremony ended. The parishioners, with ash-marks on the foreheads and a good sermon on death tucked in their hearts, departed. Some few of them may have noticed, as they passed, the exquisite, pale-faced lady who knelt in the rear pew, anxious that the church should be cleared and that the priest to whom she had sent notice should come out and indicate what would next be expected of her.

The priest finally came and called her to the sacristy, and there, in the presence of vestment-cases and candle-stick racks, kneeling on a *priedieu* before a purple-stoled Irishman, Elizabeth declared her avowed intention of becoming a member of the Catholic Church.

After the necessary preliminaries, which required somewhat more than two weeks time, she was, on March 14, 1805, formally presented to the priest by Antônio Filicchi for the purpose of making her profession of Faith, and on March 15 was received.

She signed herself with the Sign of the Cross, as her Italian friend had taught her in his mansion at Leghorn, and departed "light of heart and with a clearer head than I have had these many long months, but not without begging Our Lord to bury deep my heart, in that wounded side so well depicted in the beautiful crucifixion [a painting by a Mexican artist José Maria Vallejo which hung above the altar], or lock it up in His little tabernacle where I shall now rest forever." It was quite an international and Catholic complication.

That she was there to "rest forever" no one who will read the subsequent account of her life can deny. Despite the fact that she was to have every sort of spiritual and temporal hardship, Elizabeth's Faith was never to know the slightest quaver. She did not *dip* into the Mysteries of Christ's own religion, she *plunged*. No one ever became a Catholic more unequivocally. From this day till death, in the face of whatsoever agony, there was never again to be the slightest doubt. Her natural sincerity, always outstanding in her from the earliest moments of childhood, was supernaturalized in one wild moment of abandon, in which she surrendered without release to everything that Christ had said, and which overcame her soul in a challenge that was irrevocably accepted.

How pleasant it would have been to have seen her walking home through the streets of New York that evening, with her antique bonnet bobbing on her head, her hands folded in reverence, and her dark eyes "enlarged a little more than usual."

There had to be some dissimulation before the children, after supper had ended and they embarked upon their jollity and their games. Elizabeth remarks that night on her own "play of the heart with God while trying to keep up their little amusements with them." Anna, more discerning and suspicious than the rest, was told for her comfort that she would be taken to the Catholic church next Sunday.

Then there was the prayer, examination of conscience and contrition required to prepare for "a good confession" and "a good absolution." Whatever Elizabeth supplied in the way of sins for this sacrament, and one is inclined greatly to suspect that it was not overmuch (while still honoring the exquisite temper of the saints who enlarge imperfections to an extent we coarser folk would hardly expand our most heinous offenses), at least Father O'Brien seems to have supplied an excellent *absolution*. "It is done," exclaims Elizabeth after emerging from the box of the Sacrament of Penance, "easy enough too; the kindest and most respectable confessor . . . with the compassion and yet firmness in this work which I would have expected from our Lord himself. Our Lord himself I saw alone in this venerable sacrament."

And then there was to come the brightest of all the days of her Catholicization. It was to be, quite naturally, on an Our Lady Day, the profoundest one. Elizabeth whom *The Shepherdess* had not only conducted to Italy but to Rome's inmost secret, and in whose ears the bells of Santa Maria were ringing when she first debarked at the port of Leghorn, was, on the Feast of the Annunciation, March 25, 1805, to be made one with the Sacred Humanity which the Virgin Mary, coöperating with the love of the Holy Ghost, caused to be deposited in this world for our salvation, sacrament, sacrifice, and food. "How bright is the sun these morning walks to the church of preparations," she exclaims; "deep snow or smooth ice is all the same to me; I see nothing but the bright little cross on Saint Peter's steeple." And so on Lady-day it was all consummated.

"At last, Amabilia," she writes to Antonio's wife, "at last, God is mine. Now let all earthly things go as they will. *I have received Him.* . . . My God! to the last breath of life I will remember this night of watching for the break of day."

But day did break. The priest, belike, was very large and clumsy at the altar. And the clerk was probably listless, distracted and yawning (such is the beautiful custom of all Catholic children in the presence of great mysteries, says Hilaire Belloc) as the Mass progressed on Lady-day. But the priest, with the sure power of Orders given him, consecrated in truth, not in symbol. There were probably only a handful of worshipers at such an early hour on such a cold morning. But the altar-boy knew decisively when he was to ring the three bells for Communion time. And Elizabeth had been taught precisely when to approach the altar-rail for the reception of the great Gift she demanded of Christ.

What she said to Him with words and without them when He dwelt in her flesh in the consubstantiation of this great Eucharist, is hers and His secret. It happened in the thirty-first year of her life.

There was only one sad note, sincerely and humbly expressed in her letter to Amabilia describing the joy of her First Communion day. "My health is pitiful," she says. And well it might be!

The Outcast

And so with pitiful health, five children, a disgraced name, and no money, this gentle widow embarked on her life as a Catholic in the Spring of 1805. *Some* support, moral and financial, was hers to command. A few of her Protestant friends, notably Mrs. Julia Scott of Philadelphia, and her two sisters-in-law, Cecilia and Harriet Seton, rallied to her side. Her children were riotously happy over the whole affair of conversion, knowing that it was the only solution of "poor mama's" ill-disguised heartache. But most of her associates in New York were shocked at the event—pained, grieved, upset, alarmed, horrified, or beset with other similar emotional disturbances. It was not a nice group to walk around among or look straight in the eye. In the matter of financial resources Elizabeth had, of course, the Filicchis always to go to; and they were continually offering her sums of money to keep up her household and her station. And, as Robert Seton, biographer, remarks in his *Memoir,* Elizabeth had no false shame, and accepted gifts from them in her need, refusing to make "a show of pride, inconsistent with that true Christian charity which takes away the humiliation of dependence." But one had to be up and doing for one's self, as well, and not merely writing drafts on the Bank of Leghorn out of another's munificence, however graciously offered.

But what stood by her most at this time of tenseness and trial, was neither her friends nor their money, but

her exciting sense of inward peace. The certitude and
assurance of this gave her a rampart, a posture, even a
gaiety, that was to withstand henceforth every material
and temporal discouragement. "My soul," she writes to
Bishop Cheverus of Boston about this time, "has offered
all its hesitations and reluctances as sacrifice, with the
blessed sacrifice on the altar, on the fourteenth of March,
and the next day was admitted to the true church of
Jesus Christ, with a mind grateful and satisfied as that of
a poor shipwrecked mariner on being restored to his true
home."

It is not necessary to expatiate too much on the hos-
tility and coldness of her friends toward her at this
time. "Poor fanatic," was what they called her, and declared that her sorrows and illnesses had turned, affected
her brain. But after all what does anyone normally do
when faced with a logic which, if examined, will upset all
one's traditions in a single flash of thought? One turns
to ridicule of one's challenger. Poor human nature must
have its defenses one way or another, and it would be bad
form to let one singular emotional widow play havoc with
the religious certitudes of the whole of New York Society.

Elizabeth sometimes took the taunts brought against
her with light-heartedness and humor. "Every day some
one of the kind ladies sheds tears . . . for the poor de-
luded Mrs. Seton," she remarks in one place.

At other times her accusers drove her more strongly
into an appreciation of her present position. "She said,"
she writes of a Mrs. Livingston who came in to examine
Elizabeth's conscience, "that generally a connection with

even a Deist was not feared, while with a Roman Catholic
it was thought of with horror. I told her it was a curious
contradiction in principles which allowed every sect that
could obtain a name to be right and in the way of salvation."

But Elizabeth was a lady, high-spirited and beautifully bred, and sometimes the ridicule hit deep and hurt.
She became especially sensitive to it when her children
were humiliated. Her children took to Catholicism with
the most perfect ardor and delight. "My boys are wild
with joy when they see the cross of Saint Peter's," she
writes to Antonio Filicchi. "William is constantly asking
that he may become one of the little priests; he would
say, one of the little boys who serve Mass. 'I would
rather be one of them, mama, than to be the richest man
in the world.'" Thus, when the simple pieties of her
children began to be ridiculed and satirized it caused her
pain of the acutest kind. So much so that we find her
writing again to Antonio at a not much later date, "Dearest Antonio, prove your true love to me by exercising
your utmost power in getting my poor boys to Baltimore,
if it is possible. If you could only know the situation they
are in here, only your love for souls independent of any
personal interest in me would induce you to pity them in
the ridicule they are forced to hear of our holy religion
and the mockery at the church and ministers. Besides
their minds are being poisoned with bad principles of
every kind, which I cannot always check or control."

Antonio did try to get the Seton boys, William and
Richard, in school with the Sulpicians in Canada, but part
of the college building burned down and the classes could

not be continued. Later he placed them at Georgetown College in Washington, much to Elizabeth's comfort and delight.

In the autumn of 1805, she gives a charming picture of herself in the state of polite poverty to which she was reduced. "If you could imagine the occupation of mending and turning old things to the best account, added to teaching the little ones and having them always at my elbow, you would believe me that it is easier to pray than to write. Also I clean my own room, wash all the small clothes, and have much more employment in my present situation than ever."

By way of supporting herself, she thought to start a school for small children. This would serve a double necessity, that of earning money for food, clothes, and rent, and that of supplying her own children with the benefits of a continued Catholic education. But she was unable to succeed in any plans for starting such a school on her own.

Finally there came what seemed for a short while to be a stroke of very good fortune. A certain well-educated Englishman named White, together with his wife, had intentions of opening a school for young children, and Elizabeth was invited to join them in the rôle of assistant. The project immediately met with opposition from the New York set, who watched Elizabeth like a hawk, and undoubtedly hoped that her spirit would break and that she would return to the bosom of one of the Protestant variations of the Faith.

She describes the situation best herself. "As soon as the report was circulated that there was a school intended to the description I mentioned . . . it was immediately added, according to the usual custom of our generous world, that this Mr. and Mrs. White were Roman Catholics and Mrs. Seton joined herself in their plan to advance the principles of her new religion. Poor Mr. Hobart, in the warmth of his zeal, flew to the clergyman who had given the certificate of Mr. White's abilities to reproach him for his imprudence and told everyone who mentioned the subject of the dangerous consequences of the intended establishment. My Mrs. Sadler and Mrs. Duplex [two of the friends among her former co-religionists who were still devoted to her] finding that the scheme was likely to fall through, waited on the clergyman and explained that Mr. and Mrs. White were Protestants, and that Mrs. Seton's only intention was to obtain bread for her children and to be at peace with all the world instead of making discord between parents and children. Mr. Hobart was so very kind as to say, after this explanation, that he would use his influence for the school."

The school was opened, but it never prospered. Mrs. Seton's children went of course—why not, to her own school?—but very few other peoples' did. In a short time White ran out of money, and the school had to be given up at the end of three months.

To the honor of certain of her friends—there was always more ignorance in them than malice, and Elizabeth, for all their gossiping, compelled them to a secret admiration—it must be said that they did try while "deploring her aberrations" to seek employment for her elsewhere. This time it was in a Protestant school con-

ducted by a Mr. Harris. Mr. Harris, when the subject
was broached to him, while freely admitting Mrs. Seton's
academic qualifications, was a bit frightened of her religious affiliations, and by "a bit frightened," I mean "a
lot frightened." He knew she was the chief topic of
religious conversation in New York, and had been freely
discussed in every parlor, at every dinner table. Would
his clients undertake to boycott him for taking her on?
They might.

Weeks and weeks of conferences were necessary
before timid Mr. Harris consented to hire Mrs. Seton.
And then it was not in the rôle of a strict associate.
"They do not know what to do with me!" Elizabeth remarked. She, in another house which he would rent, and
not far from his school, and under his auspices, would
teach a certain number of children whom he would send
her. The arrangement was to last for three years, and
it might have lasted longer, had not a bomb-shell been
thrown into the midst of her friends not long afterwards.

It has already been said that three of her husband's
sisters dearly adored their sister-in-law Elizabeth. Rebecca, who was once her soul's confidante, had already
died. But Harriet and Cecilia immediately succeeded to
her place in Elizabeth's affection. Harriet, of whom more
will be said later, was, by all reports, one of the most
beautiful belles in New York in her day; in fact, was pronounced by some "the MOST beautiful." Neither in Elizabeth's conversion, nor after it, no matter what enmities
arose against her in other quarters, did Harriet abate
one inch in her adoration and affection for Elizabeth. It

was the same way with Cecilia. In January of 1806, Cecilia became seriously ill and her life was despaired of. In the crisis of her illness and all during her convalescence, she had only one request to make: Elizabeth must come and be at her side. Cecilia was very young, only fifteen at the time, and her relatives, though opposed to it, could not fail to humor her in this request. Elizabeth came, and was Cecilia's one and only consolation.

As her convalescence progressed she became more eager in spirit, and one day in her bedroom, when she and Elizabeth were alone, she sat up and whispered in her ear "I am going to become a Catholic, like you!"

Elizabeth must have known what the consequences of this action would be both for herself and Cecilia. She insisted that it must not be at once, and it must be kept a secret. The prospect was both a distress to Elizabeth and a delight. But what can one do in the face of conscience, no matter what it costs or whom it hurts? "Oh that I could take the wings of the angel of peace," she writes to Cecilia when not permitted to go to her, "and visit the heart of my darling child!"

After her recovery, Cecilia blandly announced to her family the decision she had made. A storm of rage and terror broke loose. They threatened her, they petted her, they coaxed her, they beseeched her, not to take that dreadful step. But to no avail. They locked her in her room. She went on praying and resolving. They demanded that she break all relationship with the "corruptor of her mind." She refused. A stiff soul, Cecilia, and strong and swift in her decisions.

They went so far as to threaten to deport her to the

West Indies, and made pretenses that they were buying
her passage. They even proposed obtaining from the
Legislature of New York Elizabeth's expulsion from the
city. And they could do it, for one of them, Cecilia's
sister, Mrs. Ogden, was married to a man very influen-
tial in the politics of New York state.

But nothing could stump Cecilia. Her resolve, made
in January, was fulfilled in June when she was received
into the Church and made her First Holy Communion.
Her letter to her sister, Mrs. Ogden, reveals both the
quality of her charity and her determination.

My dear Charlotte: In consequence of a firm resolu-
tion to adhere to the Catholic Faith, I left your house this
morning, and can only repeat that if, in the exercise of my
Faith my family will again receive me, my wish is to return and give them every proof of my affection, redoubled
care to please them, and submission to their wishes in
every point consistent with my duty to Him who claims my
first allegiance. Under these circumstances whatever is
the Providence of Almighty God for me, I must receive
with entire resignation and confidence in His protection.
Forever your affectionate sister,
Cecilia.

If there was one thing clear after this incident, is was
that Elizabeth Seton *must* get out of New York. She
might be tolerated there as a "poor fanatic," but certainly not as "a corruptor of youth." (Cecilia had immediately packed all her clothes and gone to live with
Elizabeth until the family storm died down.)

Two Protestant Ministers (and one of them was

Henry Hobart) went about among the persons who sent pupils to Mr. Harris's school and advised them that they could no longer trust their children to the care of such a person as Mrs. Seton. She did not know where to go. But New York was quite too much. She was being talked about, calumniated everywhere. The very next Christmas Eve—and it is impossible to think that her case was not in at least some slight measure the cause of it—a gang of Evangelical zealots tried to tear down the cross from the steeple of Saint Peter's Church in Barclay Street, and then to set fire to the church. They were prevented, says Elizabeth, by "our gentlemen" and an order from the Mayor. One of "our gentlemen" was killed in the struggle.

She thought of going to Canada, where the Filicchis at one point of distress sought to send her. But she was so frail, and the climate was *so* cold! Furthermore, Archbishop Carroll told her not to. Antonio Filicchi then thought of bringing her and the children to live forevermore in Italy. He writes to his business associates in New York, on November 3, 1806:

Messrs. John Murray and Sons,
New York.

Gentlemen: Christian religion founded on charity is so well understood by some of your neighbors as to allow them the privilege of substituting vexation and persecution to the consolation and relief due to virtue in distress. I refer to my most respected convert, Mrs. W. M. Seton, as the persecuted person. The persecutors are her relations, her pretended friends; and religion, in the shocking

inconsistency of their brains, is the pretense for vexation.
I profess, and I will evince by the grace of God, better
principles. In addition to orders left with you on my departure from America, you are requested to furnish Mrs.
Seton with whatever further sum she might at any time
call for, to support herself and her family. Perhaps she
might resolve to seek for tranquillity and retirement with
us, and we shall not be at a loss to find them an asylum at
Gubbio, or somewhere else. In that case, I would beg of
you, my worthy friends, to lend her the necessary assistance, for which due thanks and full responsibility is
most freely offered to you by,

                    Gentlemen,
                              Your obliged humble servant,
                                        Anthony Filicchi.

This is a noble letter, in the days when the grand
manner flourished so unaffectedly, and when a gentleman
could cash a cheque on the score of his bearing alone.

Fortunately (for us) Elizabeth went neither to Italy
nor to Canada. And though it was to be a year and a half
yet before she could shake from her feet the dust of the
city where she was presently so unwelcome, and depart
with her children, never to return, the Providence of God
(which had in mind what her destiny was to be in His
Kingdom precisely) though working slowly, worked
surely.

It all came about by the arrival in New York of a
Father William Du Bourg, on a visit from Baltimore.

Father Du Bourg was the President of Saint Mary's
Seminary, Baltimore. He was a remarkably intelligent,
zealous, and understanding man. In fact one can look

back and be terribly proud of the clergy in the Catholic Church in America in those days. France had sent us some of its most spiritual and cultured priests; Ireland some of its heartiest and purest; England some of its most distinguished, clearest-minded. You might be ashamed of our priests in those days for being poor, but never for not being priestly. There was not one priest with whom Elizabeth Seton came in contact who did not treat her with the paternal respect of his calling, and the courtesy of his vow. And as for Bishops, where could one find gentlemen in the whole world such as Cheverus of Boston and Carroll of Baltimore? Even Antonio Filicchi, reared in a land of Monsignori, Bishops, and Cardinals, commented proudly on the quality of the two American Bishops he knew, and recommended them with supreme confidence to his friend Elizabeth.

Father Du Bourg had come to New York on some business or other and was warmly welcomed by the priests at Saint Peter's in Barclay Street. It was at the end of the month of August in 1807. While he was saying Mass on the first morning after his arrival at Saint Peter's, he noticed, and could not have helped doing so, a most exquisite lady, clad in widow's black, who had come up to receive Holy Communion from his hands. As soon as he gave her the Sacred Host, she covered her eyes with her fingers, bowed her head, and began to cry. Even a tall, sturdy, objective Frenchman could not fail to be struck by the radiant devotion of this strange lady.

After the Mass she went up to him and asked him for his blessing. He gave it to her, but had not the slightest idea who she was. In truth he *had* heard of the rare Mrs.

Seton of New York from conversations with Archbishop
Carroll. But he did not know that this was she. Yet he
could not fail to be impressed by the agreeableness of
her manners and the air of distinction she imparted.

By the very best of good-luck he was to meet her
later in the day at the parish house in the company of his
friend Father Sibour, whom Elizabeth had come to visit.
He recognized her, of course, as the devout communicant
he had encountered that morning at the altar-rail.

They fell into conversation, and found that the one
thing Father Du Bourg wanted to start in Baltimore was
that in which she could most assist: a Catholic school.

"Would you come?" he said, knowing he had no
funds for it.

"Oh, I would come and beg!"

Father Du Bourg promised that he would "see to it."

That he did not "see to it" for another whole year
is probably not to be laid to his blame. Sudden enthusi-
asms and fantastic projects are delightful indulgences.
Over-calculating people get things done in stricter fashion, but often what they do get done is not worth over-
calculating.

Eventually (though one hates to imagine Elizabeth's
predicament with poverty and snobbery in New York
while she waited for the decision) Father Du Bourg did
fulfill his promise. He consulted with Bishops Carroll
and Cheverus and others. All agreed that starting a Catholic school would be to the very best interests of the
Catholic Faith in America.

In the Spring of 1808 Father Du Bourg again visited New York, met Mrs. Seton, and, still impressed by

the quality of her courage and patience, decided to go through with the idea of bringing her to Baltimore to open the first Catholic school.

On the ninth of June of the same year, having packed up her poor belongings, said good-bye to a few, a very few of her friends, Elizabeth gathered her three young daughters about her, took a carriage to the dock, and embarked on board a sail packet called *The Grand Sachem* for Baltimore, leaving behind her the New York that she loved, the New York that was so cruel to her, the New York which was probably not to blame. For what could it do? Stand itself on its head in order to accommodate itself to the religious excitements of a widow who had become soft-brained by reason of a visit to Italy and the death there of her husband?

The children loved the voyage to Baltimore, loved it particularly because it took seven days. They had, as usual, their songs, their family pleasantries and funs. They had their prayers. And above all, they had that one dear person whom they had never detected in a single injustice or a single insincerity: their mother.

The Nun

"Come to us, Mrs. Seton, we will help you to form a plan of life that will save your children from the dangers that threaten them. You will find at Baltimore more of the consolations of your Faith than you have yet tasted. There need be no building. You can rent a house." So wrote Father Du Bourg to Elizabeth before her departure.

Nothing but an Homeric recital can satisfy the incidents that followed Elizabeth's arrival at Baltimore until the hour of her death. But the rehearsal of technical details and complexities is not the purpose of this book; but rather to show that were it not for Elizabeth Seton, Divine Providence would have had to find some other way of supplying us with our Parochial Schools.

Likewise, there is no need to expatiate to the uninitiated on the subject of what a nun is. But, if a brief summary will do, here it is.

A nun is a lady *all* consecrated to God. She arises at five in the morning and goes to bed at about nine at night. Before she has breakfast, she has at least two hours of prayer, including Holy Mass. Every moment of the day in which she is not occupied with some necessary task, she is bettering her soul by way of spiritual reading, examination of conscience, and the like. A true nun has no worldly ambitions, desires no fame, seeks no romance, asks no reward offered on this earth. She is poor, chaste, obedient, anxious to be always the maximum of service to her sisters and to her neighbors, and the minimum of annoyance. She has the loveliest manners existent in this world, is modest, soft-voiced, invariably gay. Laughter comes to her as easily as sunlight. She is most tender in her affections, but chastity gives her a strength that is almost masculine. She talks easily and freely because the practice of contemplation has taught her what it is valuable to speak. She holds more fondness for her parents in a single thought than most daughters might in a thousand. She retains her girlishness longest, and at forty, fifty, even sixty, it is hard to guess her age. Yet she is never coy. She is as much at home discussing a new furnace for the cellar with the janitor as she is discussing the virtues of Saint Gemma Galgani with her sisters at recreation. She wears a dress that clearly distinguishes her from the world, yet has her precisions as to how it should be arranged in an attractive manner. She is most responsive to affection, but will not allow herself to be spoiled. Compliments please her, but she banishes them with a gesture, and prefers to shine in one's eyes in simple appraisal. She feels safest and most at home in her chapel, and will spend hours on end, unmindful of any distress in her back or knees, before the Blessed Sacrament. She calls Our Lady "Her Mother" and Our Lord "Her Spouse," and she has secrecies with them that no one dare inquire about or conjecture. She is beautiful in sickness, and capable of bearing pain as silently as any creature of this earth. She is modest and undramatic in her death, asks only to be laid in the graveyard of her community as "one of the sisters," and with a tombstone undistinguishable, save for the name, from any other. In death she rejoices most in those hours of her life that were lived through pure faith, in which she took Christ's revelation literally, and did not question or doubt. It usually costs but a few dollars to bury her. And there are no flowers. . . .

The Requiem Mass is said fervently for the repose of her soul, and the nuns chant the Benedictus, and weep when they are not being observed. The last thing she asks before she dies is pardon from those she may have offended or disedified, and forgiveness for any failure in her rules. She then vanishes out of this temporal scene, to be disposed of in eternity as God sees fit. She rather expects a long Purgatory, and is insistent on having prayers said for her after her death. The Sisters never fail her in this. Sometimes she will be prayed for by some old faithful of her community for fifty years or more, when it might be confidently expected that her Purgatory has long since been fulfilled. But God is very innocent, and just and holy, and human nature very frail and weak, so one never knows. . . .

This is the Catholic nun as we know her over an experience of half a century. And of her kind there were only a few scattered handfuls here in America until Elizabeth Seton arrived upon the scene. . . .

Father Du Bourg rented a house for Elizabeth in Paca Street, Baltimore, not far from Saint Mary's Seminary. It was two stories in height, not counting a tiny attic, and Elizabeth and the children adored it. With Father Du Bourg lived a married sister, Madame Fournier, and also his mother, Madame Du Bourg. These two gave the Setons a royal reception, even had one of

Madame Fournier's daughters welcome them on the first evening with a poem composed in their honor.

So happy was she in her new surroundings that she immediately wrote to Antonio: "If I ever dared ask God for anything touching our temporal future, it would be most assuredly that we might never be forced to return to New York." When summer came on and the boys were released for vacation from Georgetown College, Father Du Bourg took them in at his seminary, sparing her the added expense of keeping them at home.

In the house rented for her in Paca Street Elizabeth opened her school for girls. The Catholics of Baltimore were numerous and fervent, and so many children came at once that the house was filled. The summer passed hopefully and happily.

A great event occurred in the Autumn of 1808. Not only did plenty of children return for instruction at Elizabeth's school, but something much more interesting arrived. It seems there was in Philadelphia a very beautiful and spiritual young girl named Cecilia O'Conway who wanted to become a nun, and who felt she had an imperative vocation. But here in America we had few convents, and the most natural place for her to go was to Europe in the hope of finding admission to one of the Orders there.

Fortunately it happened that Father Babade, from Saint Mary's Seminary in Baltimore—and who had been acting for some time as chaplain to Elizabeth's establishment (indeed, had become her confessor)—was visiting in Philadelphia and he met the father of the O'Conway girl. He told him that there was something in the nature of a convent in Baltimore, in charge of a holy widow, "the admiration of all who know her," not yet a nun, but who was in the way of becoming one, and who could at least offer all that might be desired in the way of retirement, sacrifice, and good works.

Miss O'Conway immediately communicated with Elizabeth, and a few weeks later arrived in Baltimore as her first postulant.

Next thing, Mr. Samuel Sutherland Cooper, a wealthy convert studying for the priesthood at Saint Mary's, undertook to dispose of some of his fortune, bought Elizabeth a piece of property (with a house of sorts on it) in Emmitsburg, fifty miles west of Baltimore, feeling that the country was the best place to start the mother-house of a religious community, which project everyone saw was soon to come.

The year went on happily, with some hardships, but still with great promises for the future, especially when they should go to Emmitsburg.

In the Spring of 1809 another postulant arrived, again from Philadelphia, a Miss Maria Murphy. And a month later (in May) two more, Mary Ann Butler and Susan Clossy of New York. Many young Baltimore girls became interested, began reading spiritual books, examining their consciences, scrapping their beaux, and taking counsel with their confessors.

With five aspiring nuns under one roof, Bishop Carroll and Father Du Bourg held conferences and made plans for uniting them as a religious community. The first procedure was to let Elizabeth and the young ladies take simple vows to bind for a year. This they did and

Elizabeth was appointed their directress. They had as yet no permanent rule nor any permanent name. They called themselves for the time being The Sisters of Saint Joseph. They put their heads together and chose a form of religious dress. The choice fell for almost the identical costume Elizabeth had worn since the beginning of her widowhood, a black dress with a short cape. The only difference was that they also added a small white muslin cap, with a fluted border, and a black band holding it on, and fastened under the chin. It was similar to a costume Elizabeth had seen on some nuns in Italy, and admired.

It was in June, 1809, on the Feast of Corpus Christi, that this band of five sisters appeared for the first time in public, in Saint Mary's Chapel, at Mass. The place was crowded. That they felt strange both to themselves and others cannot be denied. And yet a bit proud too, undoubtedly, for there is a certain indefinable and subtle pleasure in being uniformed, as the young seminarian will tell you when he puts on his cossack for the first time, the letter-carrier when he puts on his first light-blue uniform, the policeman his first dark-blue one, and most naturally, the young Catholic girl when she is displayed in public for the first time accoutred as the Bride of Christ.

The school continued to run at full quota. In no time two more postulants came to join the community. The seventh arrival was the most astounding of all. It was none other than Cecilia Seton from New York, determined, despite the precarious state of her health—indeed, the very serious state of it—to live always with Elizabeth, and become a nun.

I think this is quite the proper point for me to say "Elizabeth" for the last time and to embark now with the title, "Mother" Seton, the name I have been anxious to use authoritatively from the beginning of this book. I salute henceforth America's first parochial-school nun with the name by which she is known to all of us, a title I first heard from one of her daughters in the Sisters of Charity when I was a very young boy: *MOTHER SETON*.

Emmitsburg

From the time Mother Seton was appointed the temporary directress of the first religious community of nuns founded in America, every month, every week, every day, is an incessant march of labors and trials on to her death. True, there will be nearly twelve years to intervene until that time, but it is to be strict soldiering all the way to her last breath. We humans must strive to do what we can with the meager strength at our command, until the last summons is sent and one goes to the Judgment of God to find out how valuable one has been in the way of Grace and character. But there must be no looking back, and in Mother Seton's case there never was any, though what incentives for looking back occurred in the course of the years to follow, we shall see.

As if it were not enough to have the ailing Cecilia on one's hands—in frightful condition of health, and yet wanting to be a Catholic nun—it was not long until another sister-in-law, Harriet, arrived at the door of the Paca Street Community, seeking refuge, shelter, companionship in Mother Seton's arms. She was not a Catholic, indeed, was engaged to be married to Mother Seton's half brother in New York, the distinguished Dr. Barclay Bayley; and Harriet was still thought of, despite the delicate state of her health—and maybe even by reason of it, because mild ill-health imparts a certain

ethereal quality—as the most beautiful girl New York
had ever seen or was ever likely to.

Harriet did not come to Baltimore to join the Catholic Church. She came because she had found the spiritual needs of her nature incapable of being cared for
apart from her adored Cecilia and Elizabeth. And, it
may go without saying, welcome she was. Everyone was
welcome in Paca Street, so long as there was room.

Mother Seton's impatience was not with Paca Street
as such; it was only that Paca Street would never be large
enough or suitable enough to accommodate the number
of young girls who were already clamoring for entrance
into her community, and who needed, if they were to be
trained properly, a place that could be called "a mother-
house," the technical term for probation places in the
nomenclature of nuns.

Emmitsburg was the site where Mr. Cooper had
bought them the property. It had the added advantage
of being only two miles away from a new establishment
started on the mountain of Emmitsburg, called Mount
Saint Mary's Seminary. This establishment was started
by a devout priest, a future Sulpician, Father Dubois, and
survives as both a great seminary and a great college until
this day. The nearness of the seminary and the priests
would assure the Sisters of a daily Mass, counsel, confessors, and spiritual instruction when they required it.

The doctors had already advised that young Cecilia
would thrive better in the country than in the city; likewise, Harriet, a girl given to fields and flowers much more
than to the indoor diversions of the city, would be refreshed there and would probably expand in strength.

With no more motive needed to drive her to a resolve, Mother Seton, accompanied by Cecilia, Harriet, her daughter Anna, and Sister Maria Murphy, set out in June of 1809 as the first vanguard for Emmitsburg, to discover what sort of mother-house Mr. Cooper had provided them with and to see what sort of place they could make of it.

The party traveled in a covered wagon, drawn by lazy horses, who walked most of the journey, having competition from the travelers themselves, who walked most of it, too. For we all get an irresistible itch to get out of a wagon and walk when we can walk faster than the horse. Inside, wrapped in a blanket, remained alone the ailing Cecilia. The distance was fifty miles, but the journey required several days. "The dogs and pigs came out to meet us, and the geese stretched their necks in mute demand to know if we were any of their company, to which we gave assent," writes Mother Seton, commenting on the journey. The natives stood in their doorways, astonished. Never had they seen such funny-looking creatures as Mother Seton and Sister Maria, garbed in the curious costumes of nuns. Nor did the natives realize that this convoy, traveling to remote parts for the glory of God and the Catholic Church, carried some of the most sought-for belles of social New York.

Poor Mother Seton, no one could fail to pity her in the trials she had to endure after arriving at Emmitsburg and the labors she had to undergo in beginning there this pioneer institution that was to be called "Saint Joseph's." It was true that Mr. Cooper had bought them property; but the house in which they were to live was not nearly completed when they arrived. So hard were their straits that Father Dubois undertook to give them his own house, and went himself to live at the Seminary. But the house he gave them—he was a hardy pioneer, and not likely to know the delicate needs of women on a missionary project—had only two rooms! Five people in two rooms! No arrangement could keep this from being a hardship.

The outdoors was very satisfactory, and it would be possible to embark on a most rapturous description of the scenery, which everyone who has ever lived in that section has praised. The climate, at least during the summer and autumn months, did Cecilia much good, and she was able to get out of bed and walk about. It also did Harriet Seton much good, in a rather different sort of way. This beautiful girl, for whom there could be no life apart from Cecilia and Elizabeth, fluttered like a humming-bird around the fringes of the Faith. When the others went to Mass, she did not go. But when they did not go "to church," she went in all alone and prayed in her own way. Around her neck she wore a locket which her betrothed had given her. It was a pledge of love, human love. It was her trial to try to reconcile it with Divine Love, which was the love her soul needed for its own personal, private moments, those periods of self-communion when nothing purely human can satisfy the insatiate spirit, either in marriage or out of it.

In our own day, no doubt, Harriet's conversion could be managed less tragically. But in her day, to become a Catholic meant nothing more or less than to be "a traitor" in every complete sense that word can convey in meaning. True, there was a text of Our Lord, clearly spoken and applicable strictly to such an emergency (and to no other) which went: "He that hateth not father and mother, yea, and his own life also, cannot be my disciple." Elizabeth had to face this text in her crisis. But this was one of those sayings of Our Lord that the sect in which Harriet was born wished were not in Holy Scripture. Before the nineteenth century had ended, this denomination, by its experts in the field of hermeneutics, would try to prove the text "apocryphal."

(It was bad business for the Reformers of the sixteenth century to hand over the Scriptures to their individual members for private interpretation. It ended up by individual members assuming the prerogative of private expurgation. They got a lot of "class comfort" out of it. But in the final outcome, as the centuries rolled on, the stature of Our Lord had been so diminished that many began to wonder—and to act on the assumption—whether He was God at all. Maybe He was only a pleasant philosopher to be easily categorized with Aristotle, Plato, even Spinoza, even Benjamin Franklin or William James.)

"Why may I not go with you to church?" Harriet cried to Mother Seton one day in July when her soul's certitudes were particularly shaken. Mother Seton replied only, "Ah, come! come!"

Eventually she did come. Out of a resolve taken on the twenty-second of July she received instruction, made her profession of Faith, and was received into what we

are pleased to call "The Fold" and which Our Lord
called, more brilliantly, and tenderly His *Pusillus Grex,*
His "Little Flock."

When Mother Seton advised her what this step
would mean in the way of suffering and humiliation and
sacrifice (and who was more expert in knowing what
it would cost than she?), Harriet replied: "I have examined all this in my own mind. I have weighed all the
consequences, but I can not remain a Protestant, and if,
as a Catholic, I am rejected even by this dear one," at
which point she touched the miniature of her fiancé
which was suspended around her neck, "I must save my
soul."

And so another Seton "went over to Rome." It is
not surprising that Mother Seton's reputation in New
York fell even lower after Harriet's conversion. Those
were the days of "proprieties," the Protestant substitute
for "dogmas." And whoever violated them was in
danger of enduring an even more violent exclusion from
"society" than the Catholic Church even faintly imagines
it can confer by "excommunication." After her conversion, Harriet lived only from July till December, 1809.
Her death, and her courage in it, were beautiful. And her
betrothed, wherever he may be now in Eternity, can be
proud of her. She became a Catholic. She did not become a nun, and she kept the locket he sent her.

When things were settled at Saint Joseph's, ten nuns
were applied to the infant "mother-house." They were
all sorts of girls, with all sorts of origins, all sorts of
cultures, and all sorts of attainments. Those who were
not strong in intellectual pursuits could cook, wash,

scrub. Those who were not good at these observances, could qualify as "scribes," "secretaries," etc. But one and all were given to charity and prayer. Here are their names: Elizabeth Seton, Cecilia O'Conway, Maria Murphy, Susan Clossy, Mary Ann Butler, Maria Burke, Catherine Mullen, Sara Thompson, Helen Thompson, Rose White. Everything Catholic has to be catholic. Ten Mother Setons would have been too much for the community. Ten Susan Clossys probably would have been, too. God arranged the pattern according to His own design. Cecilia and Harriet Seton were the exotic contributions to the bouquet.

In autumn of the same year Archbishop Carroll came to visit his new community of nuns. He was, as is well known, a member of the famous Maryland Carrolls, one of whom was a signer of the Declaration of Independence, and had no inferiority complexes about the Faith —as no noblemen have—and was a great comfort to his first small band of Sisters by reason of his benevolence, his authority, his charm.

The first winter of the Emmitsburg community was most distressing. The house promised them had not as yet materialized, despite the fact that carpenters were always coming to—and always not completing—their work.

The strictest economies had to be practised at Saint Joseph's in view of their dwindling finances. There could be no such expensive beverages as tea and coffee. Fresh meat was forbidden. Butter, milk were also among the prohibitions. They did not even have enough clothing-material to supply them their ordinary religious dress,

and some of the nuns (this an humiliation beyond com-
pare) were obliged to go around in lay attire. The
shack in which they were quartered had no glass in the
places for the window-panes. And thus fortified against
the winter, the first snowstorm arrived. In it blew
through the open windows, and the nuns had to shovel
it out again. In the face of extreme undernourishment,
they had to fight against the disease germs that winter
always distributes for the mortification of poor mortals.
Scarcely anyone withstood the emergency, and their farm-
house was reduced to a hospital in which the less unwell
nursed those who were unable to hold up their heads.
Yet their spirits flamed in the midst of these hardships.
"All hearts," wrote Mother Seton, "applied themselves
to mortification with such good will that they found the
carrot coffee, the buttermilk soup, and the stale lard, too
delicate food." This was the condition of these Catholic
nuns during their first winter at Emmitsburg.

In February of 1810 the house destined for the
Sisters was "completed." That is to say, it was physically
possible to move into it. And move in the nuns did with
all ceremony and gaiety, making much of the procession
of the Blessed Sacrament when It was being tabernacled
for the first time in their new home. For decorations in
His new altar-home God was supplied with a small pair
of silver candlesticks and a few vases filled with mountain
laurel and some paper flowers. When the school opened
—a most unpropitious time, right in the middle of winter—on George Washington's Birthday, a splendid en-
rollment of pupils was realized.

Not only that, but as the months went on, and despite the fact that to one and all Mother Seton explained the hardships of their condition, persistent applications began to arrive from young girls who wanted to become nuns and to be enrolled in the new community.

The winter was too much for Cecilia, and despite the fact that Mother Seton had taken her back to Baltimore to see if she would recover better in the comfortable home of some rich friends, she died. It was on the twenty-ninth of April, 1810. Mother was with her at the end. The last thing Cecilia did was to press the crucifix to her heart. She was buried in the graveyard of Emmitsburg, beside her sister Harriet.

In March a most astounding postulant arrived, a young girl named Elizabeth Boyle, who, though of an Irish name, was of an English family and was a convert from Episcopalianism. A well-born lady, as Mother Seton was, she came to be Mother's closest confidante and most treasured disciple. After Mother's death she became the first Superioress of the New York Community of the Sisters of Charity, the branch that still survives in the identical dress (save for a change of color in the bonnet) which Mother Seton' bequeathed to her daughters. It is recorded of Miss Boyle that she "pitched in" for the most menial tasks. Of her quality, Mother Seton was later to remark that she believed Elizabeth Boyle had never lost her Baptismal innocence in a single detail. This was high praise from one who knew her every thought. She was an expert horsewoman, and when a postulant came to Emmitsburg bringing a horse as part of her dowry, Sister Elizabeth Boyle was given the horse to ride every Saturday when she went to the churches (two of them) entrusted to the Sisters' charge, to supply fresh linens for the altar and make general preparations for the Sunday Mass. She must have made quite an impressive, if not a spectral, figure galloping down the roads of Maryland with her large black cloak wrapped about her and the white muslin cap bobbing on her head. The farmers working in their fields, or housewives pumping water at their wells, must have greatly wondered what strange sort of female it was that had been planted in their midst in the name of religion.

Building for the Future

One of the first problems Mother Seton and her nuns had to face was whether to go on as an independent religious institute—in which case there would be much prolonged negotiation needed both with her Bishop and with the Holy See—or to adopt the rule of some already established Congregation. Her French clerical advisers at Emmitsburg would be sure to recommend a French rule, because despite their genuine admiration and respect for Mother Seton and their touching loyalty to her, they were likely to have an innate suspicion of any such term as "An American Nun," presented in too sudden a form.

After considerable discussion it was found that the rule most suitable to Mother Seton's purposes and advices was that of the Daughters of Charity of Saint Vincent de Paul, a congregation already flourishing in France after having been established by him there a century and a half before. Through the medium of one of the missionary priests in this country, Father Flaget, who had gone back to visit his native France, appeal was made to the Superior-General of the Priests of the Mission of Saint Lazare, to whom was entrusted the direction of the congregation of the Daughters of Charity according to Saint Vincent's rule.

The Superior-General was requested to send to the Emmitsburg Sisters an authentic copy of the Constitutions drawn up by Saint Vincent, and if he would, please (though it was not Mother Seton who made this request), to send them two or three experienced nuns from the mother-house in France who might take over the direction of the American foundation and accustom its inhabitants to the spirit of religious life as it was practised in the convents of Europe.

Not only were the Constitutions in authentic copy sent, but the Sisters were promised, too. It may or may not be a pity that they were eventually prevented from coming to this country by the religious persecution laws of France at that time. A pity, because the quality of the letter received from one of them, Sister Marie Bizeray of Bordeaux, is an indication of the exquisite spiritual temper of her soul, her charm, and her charity. She ends her letter to the Emmitsburg community as follows: "I will conclude, dear Sisters, soon to be our companions, with the assurance of the sincere and entire devotion of your very humble servant, Marie Bizeray. 'Unworthy Daughter of Charity, Servant of the poor.' " And yet not a pity, because—being legitimately proud of our own—we are not displeased that in God's Providence the first cradle of the American Catholic Sisterhood was entrusted to an American woman as her work and hers alone.

So the French nuns did not come, the Constitutions of Saint Vincent, with some very necessary changes required by local circumstance, were adopted and approved by Archbishop Carroll, and the small American Community embarked on its course as a full-fledged religious congregation in the manner of the French. It is strange that the most decisive exemption from the original French rule had to be made in the case of Mother Seton herself. It was almost a battle. The French rule provided that in case of widows with children seeking admission to the Order, their children must first be provided for and secured a competence before they be abandoned by their mother. Mother Seton felt that she could not in conscience go on with her part of the project if she was to turn over her children to the care of another. This might be very well in France, where they could secure suitable Catholic homes, environment, and religious training, and where the temper of asceticism strained toward such a thing; but to whom in America at that moment was Mother Seton to entrust her much-loved brood of five?

By way of showing the determined temper of her mind, as a mother-and-widow problem, toward the Saint Vincent Rule, Mother Seton wrote to one of her friends at this juncture:

"By the law of the Church I so much love, I could never take an obligation which interfered with my duties to my children, except I had an independent guardian and provision for them, which the whole world could not supply, to my judgment of a mother's duty."

And to another she writes:

I never could have imagined in this world, a situation more in harmony with my disposition, my sentiments, and my taste for peace; enjoying the liberty of solitude and country life, with all the advantages of intellectual occupation. To think of living away from this valley would

seem to me impossible if I belonged to myself. But my
dear children have the first right which must ever remain
inviolable. That is why I have made a solemn engagement
before our good Archbishop, as well as with my own conscience, to prefer before all things the advantage of my
children, if it happened that I had to choose between what
I owe to them and other duties to which I was pledged.

Through the most courteous offices of Archbishop
Carroll the matter was settled, and by a special permission she was allowed to remain the legal and maternal
guardian of her two boys and three girls until her death.
Annina, her oldest, became a postulant in the Emmitsburg community and was admitted to her vows shortly
before her death. Rebecca also was received as a postulant. Catherine (sometimes called Josephine) became
a schoolteacher, was present with Mother Seton at Emmitsburg at the hour of Mother's death, and later became (strange to say) a Sister of Mercy. Richard,
her second oldest boy, "her giant," as she called him,
after some time spent at Georgetown College and at
Mount Saint Mary's College, was sent to the Filicchis to
learn banking and failed to learn it. We do not know
much of Richard in the accounts preserved of Mother
Seton's life. But we do know much of his death. He
died trying to save another's life. I shall commemorate
both Richard and Catherine later in a note. William, her
oldest boy and her husband's namesake, we can preserve
until the end of this book.

And so the years went on at Saint Joseph's. Annina's and Rebecca's deaths were the hardest trials of
those days. Burdened by these sorrows, and weakened

by relentless hard work, Mother began to burn with a
slow fever, that tantalizing up-and-down kind that results from tuberculosis, the disease that was eventually
to ravage and destroy her.

In the first election of the Community she was chosen
Mother Superior. Likewise in the second and in the
third. It was a quite obvious choice, but the saints, with
an innocence born of humility, which we proud people
cannot understand (and at times ridicule) are always
astounded at the obvious, frightened at it, ready to say
that it could not be. And this is deep philosophical in-
sight. God is the only One who *must* be.

But first Annina's and Rebecca's deaths. I think
becoming Catholics did harm to the health of all the
Seton girls. They were undernourished for long periods
at a time. Annina first enlisted as a pupil in her Mother's
academy, and afterwards begged to become a nun and was
received as a postulant. She contracted consumption, too,
had horrible chills, fevers, sweats, pain all during the
winter of 1811-1812. The winter was terribly cold, yet
she would insist on getting up and being promptly in
chapel at the first sound of the bell in the very early
morning. No trying to reason with her. She was a beautiful child, instinct with modesty, courtesy, grace, intelligence. In fact it is almost impossible to make a choice
among any of the Seton ladies, mother, nieces, or aunts
in the matter of beauty. They were of a caste all their
own.

On the morning of March 12, 1812, Annina died.
She called her two sisters in blood to her bedside, and
while gasping, choking, utterly consumed with fever, and

needing to have her lips wetted with cold water every few
minutes, asked Rebecca and Catherine to *sing!* for her.
The song of her choice was a little hymn that ended:

> For while my Jesus is my friend
> No danger can be near.

Rebecca and Catherine did try, tried very hard to
sing, and managed to get through a few notes, but no
more. Mother Seton knelt by the bedside of her angelic
child. Some of the Sisters noticed that she began to droop
as she knelt. They supported her in their arms and took
her to the chapel. There she waited until all was over.
This was the end of Annina.

Rebecca Seton loved to skate, and one winter's day,
while gliding over the ice in the pond on the grounds of
Saint Joseph's, she slipped and fell. Something in her leg
or spine cracked. And she was never able to walk again.

Every best medical aid was given her. Dr. Chatard
of Baltimore, one of the most outstanding physicians of
that city, came to examine her. She was sent to Philadelphia—at the kind expense of Mrs. Julia Scott, still
one of Mother Seton's most faithful friends in the ranks
of those she had left—and was put under the care of a
most excellent surgeon, lavished with every comfort and
care. But she pleaded all the time to be allowed to return
to Emmitsburg.

In the spring of 1815 she wrote to her brother William at Leghorn: "The spring is so far advanced that we
already hear the turtle-dove cooing, which sits on the

trees over Annina's grave." All the doctors' treatment,
all the medication, availed nothing. She came to know
very clearly the hopelessness of her condition and one
day said, by way of showing how her spirit was still un-
conquered: "If the doctors were to say to me, 'Rebecca,
you are cured,' I would not rejoice. My dearest Saviour,
I know too well the happiness of dying young, *and sin-
ning no more.*"

She sinned no more and died young, only fourteen,
the baby of the Seton children. She died in her mother's
arms.

"Think only of your Blessed Saviour, now, my darling, won't you?" said her mother, as the last dreadful
agony began.

"To be sure!" said little Rebecca, as she faintly
smiled, turned her head to one side and died.

This was the fourth Seton to be placed in the Emmitsburg graveyard. Mother Seton now began to look very
fondly to that resting-ground herself, where she would
go soon, she hoped, and never be very lonely there with
her own all around her.

But she had work to do in the meantime. She had the
school to manage, the nuns to direct, the care of the household, conferences, counsel, prayer—and one must go on
and on and build and inform these, her daughters in
Christ, with a spirit that would be equal to all the emergencies they would have to bear in the difficult life of their
choice.

Her nuns never loved her perfunctorily. They loved
her sincerely. No one could inspire their hearts with such

response to spiritual counsel as did Mother Seton. Her conferences to her daughters, by reason of their absolute clarity and sincerity, their absence of pose and all attempt at professional edification, were more treasured than the conferences of any of the clergy. When her nuns became desolate, she always found ways to hearten them. She was always so gay, so adept with a pious or humorous phrase, so intelligent, so wonderfully intelligent.

The children of the school loved her no less, and one of her chief delights was the colored children whom she loved to play with and gather in her arms.

The school flourished, the number of the nuns, despite all the discouragements that could possibly be offered, increased. In virtue of her destiny, which was to be "The Foundress of the Parochial School System in the United States," there was given her the wisdom to know that if her community was to be effective for the general needs of the Church in this country, it must expand. On February 22, 1810, the first free school was established in Emmitsburg. Another was started there on August 12 for boys. Another for German Catholic Children in Philadelphia, on October 10, 1818. And the project of starting still another in New York was begun on May 13, 1820, and completed a few months after her death.

After her death? Yes. On January 4, 1821, in the forty-seventh year of her age, God decided to call a halt, decided that she had done enough. She had been very true to Him, very courageous. That He knew. She was also very tired.

Most of her treasure was in eternity, that is, treasure

of those related to her in blood. Of those related in Grace, about fifteen Sisters, including novices, had preceded her to the cemetery of Saint Joseph's. More than fifty of her nuns survived her.

Before describing Mother Seton's death, out of the beautiful gathering of things she said and did and was and wrote during her life in religion, here are some selections revealing her different noble qualities:

Her Beauty. A certain lapsed Catholic of New York was induced by a priest to send his two daughters to Mother Seton's school. After a time he decided to take a trip to Emmitsburg himself to see what sort of a régime he had subjected them to in putting them under her guidance. Not only was his conversaion with Mother Seton so fruitful as to send him back at once to the sacraments, but he was impelled to remark to others that he would gladly have traveled six hundred miles just to see her eyes, though she should never have opened her lips to speak a word.

In the Parlor. One day Mother Seton was called to the parlor and found three persons waiting to see her, all of different standings, all on different errands. One was a priest, one a fashionable lady, one a beggar woman wanting an alms. She knelt and asked the priest's blessing; said something courteous and elegant to the fashionable lady; and extended her hands lovingly to the poor beggar woman and whispered to her an immediate word of comfort.

With Her Nuns. One of her younger nuns was obliged to go frequently to Mother Seton's room on a certain day when she particularly needed not to be disturbed. "Dear Mother," said the nun, "I fear that I disturb you too often."

"Not at all," she replied, "the sunbeams are not more welcome through my windows than your well-known step at my door."

In Correspondence. Nothing testifies so much to the remarkable power she had of expressing herself aptly and brilliantly as the note sent her by Bishop Cheverus of Boston (who received a goodly share of correspondence in his day and from persons of very great talent). He says concerning a letter written to him by Mother Seton: "I read it through twenty times!"

To One of Her Pupils. "My dear one, it is so sweet to call you so; so often I do it in my heart. . . . Now this beautiful season of Advent, do try to take its spirit . . . to think of it as the last. You have so many opportunities to love our Jesus in His poor. . . ."

A Hymn. The well-known hymn, "Jerusalem, My Happy Home, How Do I Sigh for Thee" is, as we sing it, of Elizabeth's Seton's composition. The thought and some of the words of the first stanza were borrowed from a Methodist hymnal, which in turn got it from a J. B. P. (John Brerely, Priest), a pseudonym of the Reverend Laurence Anderton, S.J. (1575-1643), who in turn got the idea of it from Saint Augustine's *Mater Hierusalem Civitas Sancta Dei,* Chapter xxv of *The Meditations;* but the second, third, and fourth stanzas are all of Mother Seton's composition, and the beautiful traditional melody is also hers. It is really quite a perfect hymn, easy to remember, general enough in sentiment not to become tiresome by repetition, and yet phrased so as to arouse warmth and devotion.

Poor Old Mrs. Lindsey. (From a packet of Mother Seton's papers.) "Poor old Mrs. Lindsey! She must see the mother. 'Come, show me your rooms,' she says, 'and your pictures—it will tender my heart.' Here is our Redeemer. 'The Lord be merciful! is it He?' dropping her curtsey; 'but where is the Holy Queen?' There, with our little Jesus. 'O! O! O!' And here is the Pope. 'Oh, bless him. I pray for him—look what he sent me,' pulling out her *Agnus Dei*. Poor old Mrs. Lindsey! yet she likes not to be thought old, nor near to death. Oh, our Jesus! But I will see only the good when tempted to *construction*."

Rebecca's Death. "Opening her eyes with weary smiles at me, she says: 'I must die, that is clear; how will you live without me, mother?' 'Mother will soon wear away and follow, darling.'

"We exchange many rapturous looks of hope. . . . Softly she sings the little words:

> Now another day is gone,
> So much pain and sorrow over,
> So much nearer our dear home;
> There we'll praise Him, there we'll bless Him,
> Ever, ever, ever more.

She leans so peacefully her darling head on mother's lap, and offers up, she says 'her poor body covered with the blood of Jesus.'"

By Herself. "To do violence to self on a thousand occasions. Renounce all satisfactions in particular. Endure the weakness of some, the murmurings of others, the delicacy of a third, yet forgetting no one!"

Our Lady. "Jesus on the breast of Mary feeding on her milk. How long she must have delayed the weaning of such a child!!!!"

Ejaculation. "I am an atom! You are God!"

Annina's Goodness. "Our Annina is so good that all who know her wish their daughters to be her companions."

Annina's Fault. "Annina has only one fault—her dangerous loveliness."

Annina's Farewell. "Christmas . . . my soul's dearest mother, oh! how much I love you. None but our Jesus knows how much. And I must be separated from you? Oh, yes, I must for a time! but I will try my poor best to be good, so that I may be united with you in eternity—and both of us united to our Jesus. . . . Oh! my mother, my soul's mother, I try to be good, yet still I fall into many faults. Oh, pray for your most loving child, but yet very bad child. Oh, my mother, this is the time of love, and Jesus can refuse us nothing. Oh, my mother, unite with me to beg for 'Thy Kingdom come.' This is written from the infirmary. Your poor, but affectionate and loving child, Annina."

About Priests. Father Simon Bruté had remarked: "Oh that priests felt for themselves as Mother Seton felt they ought to be! How much did she not suffer in witnessing their imperfections! How sorrowfully, yet how charitably did she consider their faults!" Later she herself was to write to a young priest whom she heard preach a slovenly sermon for which he had not prepared: "Sir,

that awakens my anger. Do you remember a priest holds
the honor of God on his lips? Do you not trouble yourself to spread his fire which he wishes so much kindled?
If you will not study and prepare while young, what when
you are old? There is a mother's lesson."

Again, to another who had a desire to be stationed
at Emmitsburg: "How much purer is your service where
you are, above the mist of earthly attraction; One thing
I hope you are convinced of (I as a wretched sinner know
it well), that, wherever we meet a little prop of human
comfort, there is always some subtraction of divine comfort. . . . You are remembered and loved here too much
to make it a safe place for you, unless you were sent by
God himself without the least agency of your own, and
even then I fear my brother would grow lean. Pray for
us, I pray. Your own poor Mother."

Politics. She never manifested the slightest curiosity
in regard to any affairs of a purely secular nature, and
never was known to inquire about or much less discuss
any political events. "I see nothing," she said, "in this
world but the blue sky and our altars."

Her Name for Our Lord. "Our Adored."

Bishop Cheverus' Visit. In November, 1810, the
Sisters were greatly favored by a visit from their Excel-
lencies, Bishop Cheverus of Boston and Bishop Egan of
Philadelphia. When it was told Mother Seton that there
were distinguished visitors awaiting her, she went to the
ironing-room to meet them. Upon learning the names of
her guests and finding that one of them was Bishop Cheverus, to whom she had been so much indebted for support
and spiritual advice, she fell on her knees before him,

seized his hands, bathed them with her tears, and remained kneeling for more than five minutes without being
able to speak a word.

Dear Mrs. Harper. "Dear Mrs. Harper, tell your
sweet nieces to look at the price of a shawl or veil, and
think of the poor family of St. Joseph's."

The Old Sister. Here is what an old Sister says,
describing their days at Emmitsburg: "What if the bare
necessities of life were often experienced! We had little
to eat but our appetites were so good everything tasted
savory. Our gardener, Dedderick, who had to work, got
the best of all. I sat by Mother Seton at table and many
times she ate my crusts. O she was a lovely woman,
dear!"

Mr. Cooper's Generosity. Mr. Cooper, eventually
Father Cooper, "lately sent us a barrel of honey, one of
treacle of which we make much use, a box of Smyrna figs;
one of raisins; one of prunes; and seventy or eighty yards
of pelisse flannel, besides pieces upon pieces of India muslin for underwear—that was a good thought, you must
acknowledge."

Debate. "Here we are," said an older Sister, "buried
in the midst of woods and valleys: nobody knows what
we are doing, and truly the world forgets us." To which
complaint a younger Sister replied: "My dear children,
do not grieve so much; depend upon it this valley, quiet as
it is, will give such a roar some day that the noise will
sound over all America."

Father Dubois' Opinion. "The Mother is a miracle
of Divine favor. Night and day by the bedside of her
child (Rebecca), her health has not appeared to suffer.

She held her child in her arms without shedding one tear, all the time of her agony, even more than eight minutes after her death."

To One of Her Sisters. "This is not the country for solitude and silence, but for warfare and crucifixion."

Instructions to One of Her Superioresses: in May, 1819, to Sister Margaret George upon being sent to replace Sister Rose White in New York City (the diminutives in order of appearance in the letter are for: Sister Rose White, Sister Frances Jordan, Sister Veronica Cecilia O'Conway, Sister Margaret George, Elizabeth Ann Seton, Sister Felicité Brady, and Sister Scholastica Brady): "His peace. My Margaret: Beg Rose to do all she can to get Fanny home—to let Cecil have all the time she can with her parents *as she passes.* Take care of Margaret exactly as you would of E. A. S. Mind that, my last injunction. Remember all the little things I told you in this corner about kindness to strangers in the *true spirit.* Watch carefully to make Felicité happy and the health of Scholastica who cannot bear much wet and cold, you know. I am not uneasy about her happiness or yours. You have so much to do for our Lord. May He bless you as my heart and soul bless you!"

To Father Hickey. ". . . you blessed man of God, feeding on Sacraments every morning and rejoicing your heart with the choicest Wine."

Situation in May, 1810. "We are now twelve and as many again are waiting for admission. I have a very, very large school to superintend, every day, and the entire charge of the religious instruction of all the country round. All apply to the Sisters of Charity who are night

and day devoted to the sick and ignorant. Our Blessed
Bishop intends moving a detachment of us to Baltimore
to perform the same duties there. We have here a very
good house, though a log building, and it will be the
Mother House and retreat in all cases, as a portion of the
Sisterhood will always remain in it to keep the spinning,
weaving, knitting and school for country people regularly
progressing. Our Bishop is so fond of our establishment
that it seems to be the darling part of his charge: and this
consoles me for every difficulty and embarrassment. All
the clergy in America support it by their prayers and
there is every hope that it is the seed of an immensity of
future good. You must admire how our Lord should have
chosen such as myself to preside over it, but you know He
loves to show His strength in weakness, and *His* wisdom
in the ignorant; His Blessed Name be adored forever. It
is in the humble, poor, and helpless He delights to number His greatest mercies and set them as marks to encourage poor sinners."

Annina's Word. " 'Eternity' was Annina's darling
word. I find it written in everything that belonged to her:
music books, copies, the walls of her little chamber,—
everywhere that word."

Offering to Antonio. (Written two years before her
death.) "This morning in my Happy Communion on the
Feasts of Sts. Peter and Paul, so many happy reflections
and affections flooded my heart, that the only means it
had to express its gratitude and love for the glorious faith
to which you conducted me, fifteen years ago . . . was
to ask our Lord, not only to fully recompense my Antonio for his pains and troubles in my behalf, but to

grant me further—Oh! with what fervor I asked this: to suffer in your stead whatever punishment you may have incurred for sins committed during your life, in order that I might be able to render to you some part of that immense debt which I owe you in every way."

Conflict. "I am sick, but not dying; troubled on every side, but not distressed; perplexed, but not despairing; afflicted, but not forsaken; cast down but not destroyed; knowing the affliction of this life is but for a moment, while the glory in the life to come will be eternal."

Asceticism. Everyone at Emmitsburg noticed the poverty of Mother Seton's dress, the poverty of her furniture, the absolute minimum of material things she allowed to serve her needs, her abstemiousness at table, and her exact observance of all her rules as a religious. She arose with her community at four in the morning, went to chapel, and during the full hour of meditation that followed knelt perfectly erect, forbidding herself not only to sit but even to rest her hands or arms on the bench in front of her. In this posture she could be seen every morning in the candle-light of the day's first prayers.

Temptation. Once, probably twice, she was tempted to run away from the establishment she had founded, to go off, any place, for any reason, and desert it all. She also found, being a most intense and personal individual, the most acute repulsion in obeying some of the orders of her "immediate superior." But obey them she did, with complete exactitude.

Catherine and Richard. Mother might seem to have neglected these two of her children, since there is little record to be found of any letters to either, or from either. But no. Catherine is frequently referred to in Mother Seton's letters to others as "My Kit," and is mentioned in a note to the Filicchis, after the deaths of her other daughters, in such wise: "Kitty, my only daughter, is esteemed and cherished by everyone for her piety and good conduct." Again: "Kitty (my Josephine) is delicate, lovely and pious as a little angel." Kitty eventually became Mother Catherine Seton of the Sisters of Mercy. She died at Saint Catherine's Convent, New York City, April 3, 1891, at the age of ninety-one. After Mother Seton's death, her brother William took her for a trip abroad, and she basked in the high society of England, Italy, and America. But eventually her vocation prevailed. She dedicated herself to the poor of New York, the city where her mother had had her hardest travail. Prisoners were her especial favorites, and one of her chief labors was the spiritual preparation of men condemned to face the gallows. She kept up a correspondence until her death with the Emmitsburg Sisters of Charity. But it was as a Sister of Mercy (perhaps "Charity" masquerading under another name) that she undertook to face the majesty of God to account for her ways, at the admirable age of four score and eleven.

"Richard is always my little boy," wrote Mother Seton about the younger of her sons in his childhood. "And," she adds, "in order to keep himself always near me he aspires to nothing higher than the life of a farmer."

That "her giant" was in for adventure in a big way is shown by the letter he sent to his mother in 1818 when he was sojourning in Italy. It seems a young Italian friend of his, named Rossetti, was done to death by the dagger of an enemy. As Rossetti expired he exclaimed to Richard: "Seton, do not revenge me in any way, but take care of my sister [Pauline]—show you loved me by protecting her." "At this moment as he expired Pauline entered the room," says Dick to his mother, "and judge what my feelings were."

His death might have passed unnoticed except for the vigilance of a Boston paper, which carried the following announcement about three years after his mother's death: "Died on board the brig *Oswego,* June 21st, on her passage from Cape Mesurado to St. Jago, Richard B. Seton, Esq., of Baltimore, late United States Assistant Agent at Monrovia, aged 26 years." His death was caused in an effort to save the life of a Protestant Missionary. The minister, it seems, was ill of an infectious disease. Young Seton, while nursing him, caught the disease himself and died of it.

Comfort. "They (her community) are so loving, so fixed on Mother's every look, clouds or sunshine, so depending, sometimes I would shudder at the danger of such a situation, if it was not clear as light that it is a part of the materials he takes for his work; and so little did he prepare the composition that he knows, if nature was listened to, I could take a blister, a scourging, any bodily pain, with a real delight, rather than speak to a human being—that heavy sloth which, hating exertion, would be willing to be an animal and die like a brute in unconsciousness. Oh, my Father, all in my power is to abandon and adore. How good he is to let me do that!"

Thunderstorm. "I think I can form some idea of

what death must be to one in full possession of his faculties, without the preceding weakness of nature which weighs so much on the soul. The beautiful serenity of last night at nine o'clock when I was enjoying the brightest moon and clearest sky that can be imagined, was suddenly darkened over the whole mountain, which, overhung with black, threatening clouds riven by streaks of lightning, looked too awful; and I turned to the moon in her gentle majesty over our plain with inconceivable delight, thinking to my God: The soul that looks only on you goes quietly on, and the awful storm can come and go no farther (for it seemed to be going round to the East). Dropping asleep with my crucifix under my pillow, and the Blessed Virgin's picture pressed on the heart, Kit and Rebecca fast asleep near me—what a contrast! to waken with the sharpest lightning and loudest peals of thunder, succeeding each other so rapidly that they seemed to stop but a few seconds between to give time for a sense of the danger. Every part of the house seemed struck in an instant, and the roaring of the winds from the mountain and the torrents of rain so impetuous, that it seemed they must destroy if the lightning spared. Oh, our God, what a moment! I had no power to rise or remember I was a sinner, or give a thought to the horrors of death or the safety of the children. God, my Father, in that moment so pressing, and the plunge (as I thought) into eternity the next. Oh, Mary! how tightly I held my little picture as a mark of confidence in her prayers, who must be tenderly interested for souls so dearly purchased by her Son; and the crucifix held up for a silent prayer, which offers all His sufferings and merits as our only hope. The storm abating, I recovered my self-possession, and really felt (I suppose) like one who is drawn back from the door of eternity; then going gently to the choir window and looking out to see what had become of my peaceable little queen, I saw her wrapped in clouds lit up as they passed over her with so much brightness that, at first sight, they appeared like balls of light hastening towards us, while she was taking her quiet course above them to disappear behind the mountain. There again I found the soul that fastens on God: storms and tempest rage around, but can not stop it one instant. How good it would have been to have died then, if it had been the right time! but since it was not, here I am, very happy to meet all the countenances of terror and surprise this morning, and hear the repeated exclamation: 'Oh, mother! what a night!' "

The Trial

It is true to say of Mother Seton that she died tired out. For months she had been burning with a slow but continual fever that reduced her gradually to a state of complete exhaustion. "I am going towards dear eternity so gently and imperceptibly," was the way she chose to describe it, in one of those charming utterances for which she was famous, and which she never failed to achieve right up to the very last.

When it was sunny she would go out of doors, liked to go abroad alone and muse and pray in solitude. "O God! O God! give yourself. What is all the rest?" she exclaimed to Him as she sat alone on a rock on the side of the mountain one extra-pleasant afternoon. And she declares that a silent voice of love replied to her "I am yours!"

In August of 1820 her final and complete decline began, when the ravages of the consumption seized her so violently it was feared she would die. It is true that she rallied slightly as the autumn came on, and occasionally could make brief saunters for an hour or so out of her room, but she was definitely on her final road to death. Her disease, which up to this point was chiefly manifested by fever and exhaustion, now took the form of violent pain. If her nuns must see her, they had to come to her bedside. And never once did she fail them by neglecting to give some sincere expression of endearment or charm. "Charming" is a dangerous adjective to apply indiscriminately, but it was the hall-mark of Mother Seton from the cradle to the grave. Nor did her sisters (save in her sleep) even so much as once hear her make the slightest moan to indicate the extent of her sufferings. At the very last they did, but it was when her mind was clouded for the moment with fever and delirium.

With that superb discipline by which the saints drive themselves to perpetual sacrifice, independent of the state of their bodies, or in whatever manner of illness they are placed, she began to fret about being spoiled by the kindness and attention given her in bed, and the petty relaxations she must perforce be allowed in the observance of her rule. It even worried her that she was given a comfortable mattress to lie upon.

Occasionally one or other of the pupils in the school was allowed to come in to see her, for a few moments only, and as a special privilege. Among them was a young girl who was compelled to leave the school and go and live in Europe. She took the head of this child in her hands, and though Mother Seton was not old (only forty-six), said: "If you love poor old Mother, pray for her. . . ." and as a parting greeting: "Not forever do we part, dearest. . . ." It must have been hard not to remember such a person when you grew up!

What was exactly the character of her consolations in her last months one is not able to determine. Her own statement of them had best suffice. "It is as if I were seeing the good Jesus, Him and His Holy Mother, here, continually seated by my side, under a visible form, to console me, to cheer me, and to encourage me throughout all the hours of my long and painful suffering." That revelation startled the nuns who wondered if they were referring to *real* visions. Seeing this she added, in somewhat enigmatical words: "That surprises you, and you will laugh at my imagination. Never mind! He who is our All has many ways of consoling His little atoms."

She lingered on through Christmas.

Her last Communion was made on the last day of the year 1820, Sunday, December 31. To the sister who tended her during the night and prepared her for the final reception of the Blessed Sacrament, she exclaimed: "One Communion more . . . and our eternity." The "our" is most revealing.

Although she was yet to linger for two days more, at noon on the second of January the summons was quietly and swiftly sent around the convent that Mother was dying. The nuns ran from all parts to her room. Only a few could enter, because it was a very narrow room. Those who could not, knelt outside in the corridor. Father Dubois was summoned and prepared to anoint her five senses, eyes, ears, nostrils, mouth, and hands, in the beautiful sacrament of the helpless, which is called Extreme Unction. Mother Seton lay panting on the bed, unable to utter a word. In a burst of generous enthusiasm, with a French sense of the dramatic, feeling it might console her to have any sort of spokesman in that solemn moment, Father said to the Sisters by way of preamble: "Mother Seton being too weak, charges me to say to you, at this sacred moment, in her place: first to be united, as true Sisters of Charity; second, to stand most faithfully by your rules; third, that I ask pardon for all the scandals she may have given you—that is for indulgences prescribed during her illness, by me or the physicians."

One doubts if Mother Seton did say exactly what Father Dubois reported in this oration, though there is no doubt that she said it in substance. But she was an American, not given so strictly to the French logical order; and a "one" "two" "three" enumeration of commands would be as unlike her as anything that can be imagined. However, it was a well-intentioned performance, and would certainly do no harm.

It would have been so much better if Mother had been able to speak for herself, we might hope. Fortunately enough, after an intense silence, she was able to; and in the faintest, yet clearest of voices: "I am thankful . . . Sisters, for your kindness . . . in being present . . . at this trial."

When asked what counsel she would give them as the last from her lips, she exclaimed: "Be Children of the Church. . . . Be Children of the Church."

Father Dubois administered the Extreme Unction. When this holy rite was effected, politeness, which came to her always more promptly by instinct than it did by reason, caused her to say, when he had finished, not "Thank you!" but, strangely, two slow, muddled words, "O, thankful," which seem to me to include, for all that they may have been slightly delirious, a greater extent of gratitude and courtesy than the traditional phrase could ever convey. They seem to include not only God, and the minister of His sacrament, but all the Sisters, indeed, everyone who had ever loved her or prayed for her, maybe there was included even you who read, and I who write, this unskilled memoir.

Still one more day she went on living, lying there and breathing, alone with her own thoughts of God. Father Bruté had arrived in the meantime (to give a retreat to the children of the school). He visited her, and finding her not clearly yet in her last agony, said "Perhaps you will unite with them (her children) on Sunday." Mother Seton made no reply. But she shook her head, again, and again.

Another night come on. At eleven o'clock the Sister Infirmarian, Sister Xavier, came in, after having been absent for a short time. Mother Seton's greeting to her is almost the best of all the last charming things she said. "Is that you, Xavier? How are you?"

At midnight the nuns were aroused, and came in with blessed candles. Between midnight and the hour of two, she spoke aloud and said: "May the Most Holy, the Most Powerful, and the Most Amiable Will of God be accomplished forever." It took her a long time to say it, between breaths, and gasping; but every word of this benediction was spoken.

In the very early morning of January 4, 1821, after having implored the nuns to assist her in her agony, Mother Seton begged them to say with her—indeed help her to say—the prayer of Saint Ignatius, *Anima Christi,* which she loved so well. The response, for all the goodwill in the world, was most pitiful. It went very nearly as follows:

Nuns: "Soul of Christ, sanctify me."

Mother Seton: "Soul of Christ, sanctify me."

Nuns: "Body of Christ, save me."

Mother Seton: "Body of Christ, save me."

(At this point, a certain number of the nuns burst into tears and could not go on.)

Nuns: (what remained of them) "Blood of Christ inebriate me."

Mother Seton: (unfalteringly) "Blood of Christ inebriate me."

Nuns: (How many? two or three?) "Water from the side of Christ wash me."

Mother Seton: "Water from the side of *Jesus,* wash me."

(Everyone noticed the change of word in this antiphon. And whether delirious or deliberate, it was equally significant. At any rate, at some point in the prayer, not one single nun could continue in the prayer to assist her. And Mother Seton had to go to the end of it alone.)

Mother Seton: "Passion of Christ, strengthen me. . . ."

Nuns: ". . . . ."

Mother Seton: "Oh good Jesus, hear me. . . .

Within Thy wounds hide me. . . .

Permit me not to be separated from Thee. . . .

From the wicked foe defend me. . . .

At the hour of my death call me. . . .

And bid me come to Thee. . . .

That with Thy Saints I may praise Thee. . . .

Forever . . . and ever. . . . Amen."

In the course of this prayer, Mother's daughter Catherine, the one remaining daughter she had, uttered a curious low moan and broke into a spell of sobbing beyond control. Her mother knew it. But this was not the time for retreat. If her last end must be *all* Faith, let it be so. Mother Seton quivered not an eyelash, but finished the prayer. She would find ways for consoling her Catherine, both here and hereafter. And she did find them.

Shortly before the hour of two, on that same morning, Mother Seton made a great struggle to enunciate three words. Every nun listened, in an intense hush. The ejaculation was clearly to have been "Jesus, Mary, and Joseph." But only one word came, the faintest, the most difficult, yet the most definite she had ever uttered. It was "Jesus!" The sacred name was pronounced so distinctly that all present heard.

And that was the holy death of the first Catholic sisters-school nun in America, whose sweet soul went before the Judgment Seat of God to plead not only for the remission of her own sins, but also, and perpetually, for the spiritual needs of her fellow-countrymen.

A short time later Father Bruté arrived. What he looked at on that mattress was not Elizabeth Seton. No corpse is the personality that used to thrive in it. He merely looked at the material complement that was once vivified by a spiritual and immortal soul. Though that dead body was the temple of God, the soul had left it to its normal disintegration, to its grave.

We must not blame Father Bruté for his carryings-on at the scene. Each temperament, each nation, greets death in the manner typical to it, in the fashion best suited to keep it from despair. The Irish wail, the Jews rend their garments, the French orate.

"O Mother!" Father Bruté exclaimed, waving his arms in the most disordered but unmistakable sincerity, "O Elizabeth, O faith profound! O tender pity! O recollection in the expectation of your Divine Master, and in your abandonment to Him! . . ."

And so he went on. "O heart so loving, so compassionate, so religious, so generous with all its possessions, so disinterested in everything." One doubts if anybody particularly listened to this rhetoric. Each nun kneeling there with a blessed candle in her hands, had her own expression of sorrow to dwell upon and, we hope, to comfort her and relieve her in this pent-up agony.

Father Bruté fulfilled one office beautifully. He wrote a detailed and complete account of Mother Seton's death to her very best friends in the world, the Filicchis at Leghorn, ending his letter with the touching sentence (directed to Antonio): "Pray for her, Mr. Filicchi; she loved and respected you and all your family, even to the end.—S. Bruté."

Nor can it be doubted that Antonio, who was the chiefest instrument under God in her conversion, *did* pray for her. How could anyone doubt it in view of two brief postscripts which are offered here appended, the first, in one of his letters to her; the second, in one of hers to him, both written years before.

"My Amabilia sends her love to you. . . . My brother Filippo feels for you almost as I feel. We boast both to be your champions, and we shall forget you, believe me, only when we shall be no more. Your friend and brother most affectionate, Antonio Filicchi."

"Love me too, Antonio. Pray for me. Tell Signr. Filippo to send me his blessing. Yours forever, M.E.A.S."

The Return

It is difficult to say of all love's phases which is the most beautiful. Some believe love's most exquisite phase to be that of a brother for his sister. Papini claims it is father for son. Most poets and romantics would say bridegroom for bride. But love's ideal is presented to us in the Incarnation at Bethlehem, where Mary brooded over Jesus, her Son and God.

Mother Seton had, as we have seen, many loves in her life. To each of her loved ones she gave herself completely, in simplicity, undivided. But to her son, William Seton, she gave herself not merely in love, but almost in ecstasy. There is a note in her letters to him that rises sheer clear above every utterance of her heart to anyone else in the world.

Young William remembered hardly anything of his father, being only eight when he died. He did not see his father at all in the last months of the latter's life, and, of course, not at all in death. His mother was all to him. And what a strange mother she was! Arriving at the age he could appreciate her most, at the first dawnings of young manhood, those three or four years of life in which every boy and his mother are, so to speak, farewell-sweethearts—he fetching about for a bride-to-be, she waiting for his new loved one that will seperate them —he found himself in possession of the most amazing mother in existence. Other young men of his standing

had dazzling mothers, fashionably dressed and powdered, furbelowed and bejewelled, airing their charms
and conceits at dinners, balls, soirées, and what not,
wavings fans and beset with evident reactions of delight
when gentlemen paid them compliments and were overcome by their pretty vanities.

William's mother was a pale little lady, head-dressed
with a wimple and robed in solemn black, with no adorn-
ment except a chaplet of rosary beads dangling at her
girdle and terminating in a figure of Christ crucified.
William's mother was a Catholic nun, consecrated by the
vows of Poverty, Chastity, and Obedience. William's
mother had to divide her heart among her children by
nature and her children by Grace. She was the exact and
model superioress of a religious community. Dozens
of nuns and priests, hundreds of children called her
"Mother" too. William's mother was a strange mother
indeed. And yet there went on between them a communion of love, expressed and unexpressed, that is one of the
most remarkable liaisons between woman and man ever
recorded.

She had strength, however, and bravely sent him
for two years to her friends in Leghorn, the Filicchis, in
the hopes that he would take to banking and business and
become proficient therein. But each show of courage
succumbed after its exercise in a paroxysm of tenderness
and longing, so exquisite, so abject, that one almost feels
ashamed to repeat in print some of the soul confessions
she made to him in her letters.

Banking, finance, accounts, were not for William.
And after two years of futile apprenticeship at Leghorn,

he gave up the project of business and decided to enter the navy.

There was no Annapolis in those days, nor any West Point, and so the young aspirant to a commission in the American Navy was required to enlist as a seaman on one of the United States' frigates and to learn there by first-hand experience both his trade and his discipline. So William took leave of his mother late in 1817, traveled to Boston and enlisted as a midshipman on the United States *Independence*. His leave-taking from his mother must have been most touching. We can hear an echo of their tears and embraces at parting in the letter he wrote her immediately after his farewell: "For the third time I sit down to address you a few lines. . . . I know that your dearest heart is always near me, and I can truly say that, employed or at leisure, in bed, or on my watch, your dear image is never absent from me."

The irony of their parting neither of them was to know at the moment, but they were never to meet again. After nearly a year spent on *The Independence*, William was transferred to another frigate, *The Macedonian*, and embarked on her for a two-year cruise in the Pacific. This was in 1818. There was opportunity for him, in the exchange of boats, to come to see his mother at Emmitsburg if he had striven for it. He wrote to her: "Before setting out upon such a long journey I would be most delighted, my darling, if I could spend a few minutes with you. I long for news from you; for I hope to learn that you have fully recovered from your recent illness. If not, let me know; I will do all in my power to come to see you."

But, partly because she could not stand the pain of another farewell, and partly, no doubt, because she did not want to distress him by letting him see the state of health to which she had been reduced, she refused this visit, writing in August, 1818: "My soul's darling. . . . You must not think of coming, my beloved, even if your voyage is delayed to October or November. One only thing I cannot stand in this world, that is, taking leave of you; the little while, too, you could stay, the fear of its being noticed you were absent the very moment you might be wanting. We must be firm. This world, it is certain, is not the place where you and I are to enjoy our love. Do not be uneasy about my health. . . . The sickness I had [inflamation of the lungs] leaves a long weakness, but there is nothing alarming, my love. . . ."

And so, in the one time during the three years' separation when they could have met again, they did not, with something of Spartan courage to set them against it, agreeably mixed with Christian weakness.

At any rate, in his wanderings around the world, on his various boats, William was followed by a series of letters from his mother into which was poured such a torrent of tenderness as to make Monica's tears over Augustine seem almost mild in comparison. If there have been any more rapturous love-letters from a mother to a son ever penned, I certainly have never come across them. Nor were they mere "doting" letters, exuberant with maternal excesses in which William was merely passive and allowed himself to be spoiled. Theirs was a perfect communion of love, and in his letters in return he could match her phrase for phrase, thought for thought, love for love.

And what is most surprising in Mother Seton's letters is that her heart could keep its flame burning in the midst of such weariness, exhaustion, and such numberless duties. The abscesses on her lungs never really healed. She was undernourished, overworked (this because of her zeal, not because of any importunity on the part of her nuns); she was pale, middle-aged, declining day by day into the grave. Nor did she have time ever, with the countless tasks incumbent upon her in the ruling of her community and the running of her schools and orphanages, to sit down and *moon* over her letters. They simply poured out of her heart in the few moments she could gather now and again to send William a greeting. And these letters, though possessive in one sense, are in another, very models of unselfishness and self-forgetfulness. One thing and one thing alone she prayed for in regard to her son: that he would keep his Baptismal innocence, hold firm to his Faith, save his soul. Every other consideration of herself and of him was lost in this one concern. William's welfare was her obsession, just as it had been for the older William, his father. She used every instrument of charm and fascination she possessed to make virtue attractive to him. God immanent and near, and salvation important. Excerpts from letters written during the three years of William's wandering will show how tactfully and tenderly she keeps his eye clear to the mark of his eternal destiny:

"My Soul's darling. You go, so adieu once more!

. . . You must fill a station and take a part in our life of trial, and all your mother can beg is that you keep well with your good pilot, and, as says old Burns, the correspondence fixed with heaven will be your noble anchor. To go when you can to the sacraments as a child to his father will be the main point for that. . . ."

"Now, my love, I must hope that you are safe in your berth. Your little ship left behind has had cloudy weather and dragged scarcely three knots an hour. Good Madam Reason argues, insists, and shows so plainly our order of duty that we must separate, and yet with all that she can say, I miss you to such a degree that it seems my own self remains but as a poor shadow and its dearest part is gone. My best comfort is to be continually begging God to bless you, or to be guessing and supposing where you may be. . . ."

"Last night I had you close where you used to lie so snug and warm when you drew the life stream twenty years ago, and where the heart still beats to love you dearly till its last sigh, which even then will love you best of all. . . ."

"Unite your dearest heart well with mine every morning at least—this I earnestly beg. You do not know how it will help in some of the peculiarities of your situation and how much it will supply for what is so much easier for me than for you. . . ."

"Your mother ought to say many things, but can say nothing. Look up to the pure heavens in your night watch, my beloved, and you will hear what that soul would say to you, what our beloved ones gone would say too. . . ."

"My own William,—I have written you every way I could devise,—New York, Baltimore, Boston, etc. The most welcome of all letters from Valparaiso we received the middle of July, and we hardly dare hope for another yet. . . . How we think of you, delight to speak to you, listen to every wind as if it might reach you; our thousand fears and hopes, all so inexpressible, and counting the days and weeks as they pass in view of that dearest one which will bring you again to us. Oh my dearest William, will it, can it be that once more you will come to your little valley? . . . Every time the clock strikes I so earnestly bless and call down blessings on you. Oh, my love, dear love, love me—you know how and by what proof. When you are passing Cape Horn again you may be sure of my poor, wild, mother's prayers—my only, only comfort, night and day, beloved. . . . What could ever force me to live separated from you, but the one adorable Will? I would go the world over in any disguise,—hidden even from yourself—to be only in the same vessel and share the same dangers with my William. Oh, my soul's dearest, deny me not the only meeting where we will never part. You know well, it depends on yourself. The agony of my heart, as I carry your beloved name before the Tabernacle, and repeat it in torrents of tears, which our God alone understands, is not for our present separation; it is our long eternal years which press on it beyond all expression. To lose you here a few years of so embittered a life, is but the common lot; but to love as I love you, and lose you forever—oh, unutterable anguish. A whole eternity miserable, a whole eternity the enemy of God—and such a God as He is to us!"

And so on and on for three years went these heart-rending missives from a slim, small nun in Emmitsburg to her sailor son in the various ports of Asia. It is almost impossible to make a choice from them for they all measure up to the same passionate, exquisite intensity. And there were not merely three or four, but dozens. The reader and I are far too worldly-wise not to know the chiefest concern in Mother Seton's heart for the son she had reared in such innocence and purity. And yet not once by direct statement is it alluded to. "Unite your dearest heart well with mine every morning at least—this I earnestly beg. You do not know how it will help in some of the peculiarities of your situation and how much it will supply for what is so much easier for me than for you. . . ." Was there ever a statement freighted with so much discernment and reticence? "Chastity," says Father Martindale somewhere, "is not negative and white like snow. It is positive and white like fire." It does not resist. It attacks, and burns out its adversary.

A young handsome boy of twenty, set in a milieu of young midshipmen, of spurious morals and great temptations (and God must pity the trials of these poor young men in the monotonous routine of ship-board-life) is an easy target for the kind of sins one likes to think one can commit and forget. Girls were sitting on every dock waiting for ships to come in that would deliver them money and temporary affection. Sailors *needed*, almost, to get drunk to salvage their sanity from the interminable sameness of a sea-voyage. Innocence has its own wisdoms, as witness Our Lady's clear, shining reply to Gabriel:

"How can this be since I know not man?" Though the phraseology of this reply is angelic, its meaning is unmistakable. Mother Seton was not in the least averse to her son's falling in love or getting married (later he *did* marry, and one of his sons became an Archbishop) ; but she was judiciously worried, as well she might be, lest in the interim that awaited the arrival of his honorable bride, he might fall into the casual amours which so often result in a disgust for all women forever after. And she sought to supply him a rampart in the meantime by the chasteness of her own heart and the solicitude of her own vow. Nor did he fail her.

Did William Seton ever speak to the other midshipmen about his mother? Probably not, to any detailed extent. How could one ever explain her? How could one tell one's fellows about having a mother who was a Sister of Charity, the Superioress of a religious community, a nun? Yet they must have noticed a mysterious aloofness in him, especially when the mail packet arrived and he was delivered one of her letters. And in the general swapping of letters, in which practice I believe sailors indulge, was there any tattooed midshipman aboard who received or could receive from any mother, sister, sweetheart, *such* letters as he was constantly receiving from his cloistered loved-one in Emmitsburg Valley? Who could match her in point of tenderness, sympathy, understanding? Who could even approach her in point of style, charm, literature? William knew that a game was being played against him all during the voyage of *The Macedonian,* to keep him close to his prayers, his sacraments, his commandments. It was a game in which he delighted, and reciprocated as much as any mother's heart could wish.

But the climax must come and did come. *The Macedonian* completed its two-year voyage and sailed into the port of Boston. From there William had only one objective: the convent in Emmitsburg, his mother's eyes, and her heart on which to rest his head. In a letter to his mother, he tells what he will do.

"No delay," he writes, "from Boston I post it to New York, shake hands with our friends there, then on to Philadelphia. Here I debate a moment whether to go by steamboat to Baltimore or to take the stage through Lancaster to Gettysburg. The latter route is ever dear to me in my remembrance, having traveled it in such sweet company [hers]. At Gettysburg I take a private conveyance and arrive with a beating heart in Emmitsburg. Then to St. Joseph's. The scene there may be felt, not described."

The Macedonian was to stop, after Boston, at the ports of New York, Philadelphia, and Baltimore. But this was all too much delay for William. He must debark at Boston, get on stage-coaches, on carriages, on any sort of conveyance that is swifter than a ship, to bring him in the quickest possible time to the arms of his mother. In sight of Boston Lighthouse, while his ship was waiting entrance, he dispatched another letter to her.

"My dearest mother: My dearest desire seems about to be fulfilled; happiness, like a star which gleams through a wild and stormy night, appears to rise before my eyes. But, alas! the horizon does not clear, and my poor star trembles, as if it would be obscured by clouds. You can imagine with what anxiety I await the reception of the first lines you will write me. Your last letter was dated the month of May, 1820. That is more than a year ago. I dare not let my thoughts rest on the changes a year may bring. Do write me soon and tell me how you are. Embrace Kitty for me. My regards to my friends at the Mountain. I keep my long stories for the time when we shall be together; or rather, to speak truly, I feel my heart so full at this moment that I can say no more."

And so, on a certain warm spring day in June, 1821, William's frigate dropped anchor in Boston Harbor. And the dockmen standing on the wharf nearby must have been surprised to see a young midshipman immediately put out for land in a small boat, leap out of it as soon as it had been moored, and with extreme impatience, while shifting the knapsack on his back nervously, terribly intent on getting somewhere in a hurry, inquire the shortest route to the stage-coach for New York. The directions were given him, and off he bounded on the run.

The trip was sure to be a tiresome one, taking at least all of five days, and the excursion, whether by coach or wagon, was full of more jolts and halts and delays than anyone even in his very best nerves would bargain for. Then there were garrulous fellow-passengers anxious to fill one's head with unnecessary information, anxious to distract one from the single thought focused in one's mind as the horses galloped or walked, as they were changed at the relay stations, or stabled for the night at inns, where one had to loll, be plied with questions, uselessly admired, and, of course, delayed, by way of an eight hours' ses-

sion in a feather-bed where one did not, could not sleep, in
the face of the important advance still ahead.

New York! No delay there. Better to hurry on to
Baltimore by the first sort of vehicle one could command.
Four more days to Baltimore!

In this snail-like progression of hooves and wheels
William fidgeted, yawned, loathed, and resented. It was
not the days of cigarettes when one could get some ap-
peasal of nerves by smoking interminably. He tried to
sleep but couldn't, and finally didn't want to.

Baltimore! Some refreshment guzzled at the most
convenient place, and then wildly gesticulated inquiries as
how quickest to get to Emmitsburg, still fifty miles away.
A coach part way, a hitch-hike on a wagon for more of
the journey, a hired private carriage for the rest. But
always horses tiring of the run and dropping into the insufferable, slow walk of horses, and always inns where
one must rest. Something electrical in the air kept telling
him that it was imperative to hurry, to press on, to avoid
the small talk of the curious, to get by all ways and means
swiftly to the convent where his mother was waiting for
him.

There was an interval in the last day of his journey
when he thought not to reach her before nightfall. But
the horses rallied and succeeded on this point. No matter
when he arrives.. He can come even in the middle of the
night, and she will be waiting!

Emmitsburg at last. "Here! Take your fare, and
keep what's over!" Out of the carriage he leaps, and
then down a side-street on the run. Southern families sit
on their verandahs, and young belles stare at this hand-

some midshipman racing through the streets of Emmitsburg.

At last the sight of the Saint Mary's Mountain. His mother's convent is nestling in the valley only two miles below. How glad the Sisters will be to see him. There will be what a supper! He will be the center of all eyes, the object of all interest for days and days.

Up the hill, not walking, but on the run. Yes, full speed all the way. Then down the hill! If he meets his mother breathless, it will all the better tell her of the delirious desire he has to see her again, and take her in his arms.

There is the convent gate, the spire! Some Sisters are standing in the doorway. Why do they not run out to meet him, as he supposed they would? And where is his mother—not waving in the midst of them?

Father Bruté is approaching. Why does he not run, too? Is this not the wildest moment of excitement for any boy in the world, to be seeing his own nun-mother after three painful years of separation?

Father Bruté has something in his hand. He comes up to William, but dares not look at him. . . .

Truths are best told by gestures, sometimes. And when an old French priest, whose eyes are streaming with tears, hands you your own letter to your mother, with the seal unbroken, in one sudden moment, the world breaks around you shattering everything you have hoped for, lived for, dreamed of. . . .

It was just at eventide. The night Angelus was ringing, and all his mother's nuns were dropping to their knees to repeat again the Angelical Salutation, as William

Seton walked into the garden graveyard of Saint Joseph's Convent at Emmitsburg.

He did not cry. He was composed, stalwart and erect, for there were three years of sea discipline already in his bones. Sailors do not cry. They cannot afford to. The ship sails at any moment. Tears are for the dock; but a right hearty cheer is for men set free in the open sea!

But anyhow, he saw some graves there he knew well. There were the graves of his two aunts, his father's sisters, Harriet, and Cecilia. There were also the graves of his own young sisters, Annina and Rebecca.

And his eyes turned toward one other grave. The sods had firmly settled upon it because it was nearly six months old. A plain wooden cross was planted at the end of it, just where the length of a little body might be assumed to terminate.

The inscription on the cross read:

SACRED TO THE MEMORY

OF

E. A. SETON

FOUNDRESS

William looked at it for a long, a very long time. Then he fell to his knees, and bending, pressed his lips against the soil that covered his love, his mother—our saint and our country's glory.

THE END

Father Leonard Feeney, M.I.C.M. was born in Lynn, Massachusetts "on the night the battleship *Maine* was sunk," as he remarks in this book. He was educated in seminaries in the United States and Europe, and was ordained a priest in 1928. He is the author of more than a dozen books of prose and verse, and his writings have long enjoyed wide popularity in Catholic circles. A former professor of Rhetoric and literary editor of *America* magazine, Father Feeney has for many years been superior of St. Benedict Center, first in Cambridge, and now in Still River, Massachusetts. In 1949 his insistence on the necessity of membership in the Catholic Church in order to obtain salvation brought him into conflict with ecclesiastical authorities. Without pronouncing on the doctrinal controversy, Pope Paul VI authorized the removal of all ecclesiastical censures from Father Feeney in 1972.

In a famous sermon delivered some years ago in St. Patrick's Cathedral Father Feeney expressed the hope that the United States would one day have a "St. Elizabeth of New York." The canonization of Mother Seton, therefore, comes as the fulfillment of a life-long desire, and Father Feeney is especially pleased to be able to mark the occasion by publishing a new version of his biography of the saint.